# To the End of the Age

## Christ's Presence in the World

Aaron Simms

*To the End of the Age*

Second edition - Copyright © 2014 Aaron Simms

First edition - Copyright © 2012 Aaron Simms

All rights reserved. No part of this publication may be reproduced, distributed, or transmitted in any form or by any means, including photocopying, recording, or other electronic or mechanical methods, without the prior written permission of the publisher, except in the case of brief quotations embodied in critical reviews and certain other noncommercial uses permitted by copyright law.

ISBN: 0692213945
ISBN-13: 978-0692213940

Published by St. Polycarp Publishing House
info@stpolycarppublishinghouse.com

Printed in the United States of America

---

Scripture quotations, unless otherwise noted, are taken from The Holy Bible, English Standard Version® (ESV®), Copyright © 2001 by Crossway, a publishing ministry of Good News Publishers. All rights reserved. ESV Text Edition: 2011.

# DEDICATION

To my wife Amy and my children Molly and William, blessings from God.

# CONTENTS

| | |
|---|---|
| ACKNOWLEDGMENTS | i |
| PREFACE | 3 |
| INTRODUCTION | 5 |
| 1 OUR TRIUNE GOD | 16 |
| 2 CREATION | 34 |
| 3 MARRIAGE | 48 |
| 4 GOD'S PROMISES | 59 |
| 5 FREE WILL AND GOD'S WILL | 67 |
| 6 SUFFERING AND COMFORT | 81 |
| 7 BROKENNESS AND RESTORATION | 92 |
| 8 LIFE AND DEATH | 102 |
| 9 HEALING AND COMPASSION | 111 |
| 10 CLEANING UP | 121 |
| 11 CHURCH AND WORLD | 128 |
| 12 WORSHIP AND WORK | 140 |
| 13 LIFE IN THE WORLD | 151 |
| 14 LIFE IN THE CHURCH | 168 |
| 15 OUR WORD AND GOD'S WORD | 179 |
| 16 OUR CHRISTIAN HOPE | 187 |
| 17 TO THE END OF THE AGE | 197 |
| CLOSING THOUGHTS | 206 |
| SUGGESTED READING | 209 |

# ACKNOWLEDGMENTS

Thank you to my wife Amy and my children Molly
and William for all your love and support

# PREFACE

As Christians living in the world, we are confronted with many issues. We often face a sense of brokenness and struggle when life does not seem to be as it should. We deal with matters of life and death. We wonder about the relationship between body and soul. We wrestle with the interplay of our faith and politics. We are confronted with environmental issues and wonder how creation fits into the picture of God's plans for us. Ultimately, we are concerned about how we are to live our lives in this world in the light of what God has done for us through Jesus Christ. In addition, we also often ponder just where Jesus Christ is now and what role he plays in the present world.

These are the types of issues that this book deals with. Each chapter deals with a particular issue, and the discussion of each issue is guided by a set of passages from the Bible. Thus, each issue is considered in light of these "guiding passages," so that the discussion is grounded in Biblical truth. The writing is in more of a conversational, first-person tone that befits "proclamation," rather than simply an academic treatise of theology. Hopefully, this will help the reader see the applicability and all-encompassing nature of the Christian faith.

Some of these Biblical passages and the ensuing discussion will be challenging. Indeed, it is impossible for them not to be thought-provoking when dealing with the complexities and imperfections of life. Many of the discussions will run counter to "pop-Christianity" that is prevalent in American culture. However, each discussion will be centered around

God's Word revealed to us in the Scriptures and Christ's continued presence in this world. Thus, what is to come out of these discussions is that we live in a world that, although fallen and broken and not as it should be, is a creation of God that He continues to care for and has plans to restore. So, as we live out our lives in this world we live knowing who we are and how we fit into God's plans. We also live with Christ's presence, because He has not abandoned us. In Matthew 28, after commissioning us, his Church, to make disciples of all nations he also promised us, "I am with you always, to the end of the age."

Therefore, this book will provide the grounding for understanding the who and how of our relationship with God and with the world in the light of Christ's continued presence. For this is ultimately the issue with which we are dealing: Who are we, how are we to live in this world, and what hope do we have? God provides these answers in His Word that He has given us, and this book explores this Word to see that we can enjoy life in this world as we live in the light of God's grace and mercy through Jesus Christ.

Readers familiar with Lutheran sermons will recognize familiar themes, while Christians from other strands of the faith will be introduced to Lutheran concepts that are useful in holding up Jesus Christ as the one through whom we have forgiveness of sins, restoration, healing, and salvation. Thus, each chapter, indeed the whole book, is Christocentric. That is, all of the issues find their answer in Jesus Christ, "For all the promises of God find their Yes in him. That is why it is through him that we utter our Amen to God for his glory" (2 Corinthians 1:20).

# INTRODUCTION

Framework

In order to better understand the discussions which follow, a few distinctions must first be put forward. As we contemplate issues relating to God's Word, our role in the world, our place before God, and God's will, we have to know a little something about how to parse God's Word which He has revealed to us through the Scriptures. The Bible contains a great many words and events which have to be considered within some sort of framework in order to faithfully and correctly understand God's self-revelation of Himself to us.

The categories outlined below provide such a framework for interpreting God's Word. These are often called "Lutheran distinctives," since the Lutheran confession of Christianity often makes use of these categories. However, these categories are, in fact, "Christian distinctives," because they uphold God as our holy Lord who graciously justifies sinful humanity in His sight through the work of Christ on the cross and empty tomb.

Therefore, the short discussions below on these main interpretive categories, or "distinctives," will provide the framework for the discussions in the following chapters. Throughout the rest of the book these categories will be fleshed out more fully as they are interwoven within the ensuing topics. Not only will this help to make sense of God's Word, but it will also show that God has always been justifying and saving sinful humanity one way, and that way is through His Son Jesus Christ (cf. John 14:6).

## Law and Gospel

God's Word comes to us in two ways; it is either a command or a promise. That it, it is either threatening us with God's punishment or giving us God's grace. It is either condemning us or saving us. It is either killing us as sinners or bringing us to new life. We therefore view God's Word as two-fold; it is both Law and Gospel.

The Law is God's commanding, threatening, condemning, and killing Word. The Law has three uses: maintain outward order in the world (i.e. it is a curb to sin), reveal to us our sinful natures (i.e. it is a mirror to show us how we really are), and provide us God's will for us (i.e. for redeemed sinners, it gives us a guide as to how we are to live in the light of God's redemption of us).

God has written the Law on all our hearts, believers and non-believers alike, so all people have some knowledge of God and His will for our lives. This is often called "natural Law," because all people by nature have it within them. The Law given to Moses by God on Mount Sinai is often called the "revealed Law," because through it God clearly reveals what He has written on our hearts. However, all people, even if they have never heard of the Ten Commandments, have an inkling of the Law due to "natural Law" and are therefore without excuse (cf. Romans 1:20, 2:12-15).

The Gospel is God's promising, giving, saving, life-giving Word. It is the Word given to sinners who have been crushed with the weight of the Law and brought to repentance. It is the Word of promise that our holy Lord God does not intend to leave us in sin and death. It is the Word of grace that says that Jesus Christ, God's Son, died for our sins and rose for our justification (Romans 4:16-25). However, unlike the Law which everyone can know, this Word of Gospel is a mystery which must be revealed, because it is counter to what we would expect. Due to our fallen nature, we can not know the things of God through our own reasoning, so these things must be revealed to us (Romans 16:25-27).

The Scriptures as God's Word contains both Law and Gospel. His Word comes to us in this two-fold form. God condemns sin and sinners through the Law and then raises sinners to new life in Him through the work of Christ. Thus, the Law serves the work of the Gospel. The saving work of the Gospel is what God wants to do; it is called His "proper" work, because God "desires all people to be saved and to come to the knowledge of the truth" that is in Jesus Christ (1 Timothy 2:4).

However, in order to bring sinners to repentance so that they will trust in His grace and mercy given through Christ (i.e. so that they will believe the Gospel), God also uses His Law. This is His "alien" work whereby He crushes sinners to bring them to repentance, removing any sense of self-righteousness and pretension from them, so that He may show them His mercy through the Gospel and they receive it as the unmerited gift that it is. Thus, the Law is used to show a sinner his sins and bring him to a recognition of the truth that he can not save himself through his own efforts of works. Then, the Gospel is used to show the sinner the one through whom he has forgiveness of sins and reconciliation to

God; the Gospel gives the sinner Christ crucified and risen as a free gift of God's grace.

## Two Kinds of Righteousness

Related to the Law/Gospel category is a further distinction between our "two kinds of righteousness." As human beings, we have a relationship with God as well a relationship with other people. That is, we have a vertical connection with God and a horizontal connection with the rest of the world. Thus, we stand in relationship before God and before the world.

In our standing before God (i.e. the vertical dimension), we must rely on God's grace given us through the Gospel of Christ, because our own works can not bring us into a right relationship with Him. Thus, our righteousness before God is a gift from Him to us. It exists outside of ourselves and exists instead in God. By His grace, God clothes us with the righteousness of Christ, which is His gift to us due to Christ's death and resurrection. Thus, our righteousness before God is not due to anything we have done, but is rather due to what Christ has done. We can stand before God only because of the gift of Christ's righteousness that covers our sins.

In our standing before the world (i.e. the horizontal dimension), we do, however, rely upon our own works to be "righteous." That is, we do "good things" that help other people and God's creation and we are therefore considered "righteous" in the eyes of the world due to these works. Thus, even non-Christians can be considered good people in this dimension as they do works that are helpful and beneficial to life in this world.

However, where we make a mistake is when we try to apply the working of the world in the horizontal dimension to our relationship with God in the vertical dimension. Thus, if we try to apply our worldly righteousness to our relationship to God, rather than relying on the gift of Christ's righteousness, we stand naked and condemned in our sins. In our standing before God we can not rely on our own works, but must instead rely on Christ's work that he did on our behalf (cf. Titus 3:3-7).

The wonderful freedom, then, that we have as Christians is that God has already redeemed us from sin and death and evil through the actions of Christ on the cross and empty tomb. God has already done it all for us through Christ; there is nothing left for us to do to fix our relationship with Him. Thus, we are freed to work for the benefit of our neighbor (i.e. all people) and God's creation. We can focus on bettering this world, because we have the sure confidence that God has already reconciled us to Himself through Christ. So, God has no need of our works, but our neighbors do, and we have been freed to work for their benefit since God has already done everything necessary for us to stand in His presence.

## Two Realms

A further distinction is that between God's "Two Realms," sometimes called "Two Kingdoms." As the Almighty Lord God, Creator of all things, God is in charge of everything. He is Lord both of the Church as well as all Creation. We therefore make a distinction between God's "Left Hand Realm" and

His "Right Hand Realm."

God's Left Hand Realm is civil government and institutions that God has ordained in order to keep order and peace in the world. God gives His Left Hand Realm the Law as its primary instrument to use to keep this peace and order (see the discussion on the first use of the Law above concerning its function in restraining evil in the world). Thus, civil government is charged by God with using the sword of the Law to punish wrongdoers, enforce contracts, and protect its citizens (cf. Romans 13:1-7)

God's Right Hand Realm is the Church that spans space and time. God gives the Church the Gospel as its primary instrument to use to forgive sins and restore sinners to God (see the discussion above about God's "proper" and "alien" work). Thus, the Church is charged by God to absolve sins and bring people into the nation Israel, which is God's redeemed people in whose midst He dwells.

There is also a further distinction between what we might call the "hidden / universal Church" and the "visible / local Church." What this distinction simply means is that in this world we see visible, local manifestations of the Church, such as denominations and congregations. These are filled with both true believers as well as unbelievers, and it can be difficult or impossible for us to tell them apart. But, we hold as an article of faith that there is one single, holy, universal Church that spans place and time and that is known to God because it is populated only by true believers (see the third article of the Nicene Creed). Thus, when this book talks about "Church," the "one holy catholic and apostolic Church" confessed in the Nicene Creed is what is in mind, not the local manifestations of Church such as congregations or denominations.

The point of this distinction between God's Left Hand Realm of civil government and His Right Hand Realm of the Church is that God is in charge of all things and that He uses all things for the benefit of His creation. He keeps order in the world through civil government and forgives sin through the Church. Both Realms have their own important roles to play in caring for God's creation, and both Realms are "good" in that they have been ordained by God. In addition, both Realms should be mutually supporting. That is, civil government keeps peace and order in the world to allow the Church room to operate, while the Church spreads the Gospel and reminds civil government of its proper role and sphere of influence, calling civil government to account, at times, when it overextends its given mandate. Thus, there is not really a "separation of Church and state;" rather, both exist under God's rule with their own given roles to play.

## Hidden God and Revealed God

As God, the Lord has the prerogative to reveal what He will as well as to keep hidden what He will (cf. Deuteronomy 29:29). Thus, God reveals certain things, while keeping others hidden. Thus, there is a distinction between the "hidden God" and the "revealed God." This is not to say, however, that there is more than one God. It simply means that there is the God whom we know, because He has revealed Himself to us; there is also the God whom we do not know, because He has not revealed certain aspects of Himself to us. There is one God, but there is the revealed side of Him as well as the hidden side. We can know His revealed will, but can not know His hidden will.

To put it in earthly terms, a child knows his father mainly through what his father reveals of himself to him. The child can discover certain things for himself about his father, based on what he sees his father do. However, more detailed knowledge of his father must be obtained through the father's self-revelation to his child.

Thus, with our Heavenly Father, we can discover certain things about Him through what we observe. In nature we can see that God created all things and that He is Lord over creation and history. However, we can not see what type of God He is. Is He loving or vengeful? Does He care about His creation or does He leave it to its own devices? This type of "general revelation" that we observe about God is not enough to tell us what type of God we have.

Therefore, we must rely on what God reveals to us of Himself; this is a "special revelation" by which He tells us who He is. In the Scriptures we see God continuing to reveal Himself to us, and this self-revelation reaches its zenith in Jesus Christ who is the Son and very image of God (cf. John 14:8-14; Colossians 1:15). God reveals Himself and His plans for us through Jesus Christ. Thus, we know God only by knowing His Son, because it is through the Son that God reveals Himself to us (John 14:6). Through His Son, we know that God is redeeming sinners to Himself and restoring His fallen creation. This is what God clearly reveals to us.

Certain things, however, God does not reveal, but instead keeps hidden. He has not revealed when the Last Day (i.e. the resurrection and judgment) will come, nor has He revealed why some are saved and some are not, nor has He revealed all the answers to our questions. Thus, we are called not to delve into the hidden things of God, but to content ourselves with the God who has revealed Himself through His Son as our loving and gracious Lord and Savior.

## Justification and Sanctification

Justification is the act of making something "right" or "justified." Sanctification is what happens after justification. In the context of our relationship with God, justification is how God makes us "right" with Him while sanctification is how God works in us after having justified us in His sight.

Ephesians 2:8-10 speaks of the interplay between justification and sanctification. In this text St. Paul writes: "For by grace you have been saved through faith. And this is not your own doing; it is the gift of God, not a result of works, so that no one may boast. For we are his workmanship, created in Christ Jesus for good works, which God prepared beforehand, that we should walk in them."

Verses 8 and 9 speak of justification, saying that we are saved by grace through faith in Christ; what is more, even this faith is a work of God. God has justified us in His sight through the work of Christ and brought us to faith in Christ's work. Then, our good works flow out of this faith as God works in us to produce the fruit of faith. Jesus in John 15 speaks on the same subject of justification and sanctification, stating that he is the vine and his disciples are the branches and that all they do flows out of their identity in him.

Thus, God has done it all for us. He has saved us, justifying us in His sight through Christ's work on the cross and empty tomb. Now, having saved us, He also works in us to produce good works. These good works do not justify us in His sight, though, since we are saved not by anything we do, but rather by what God has done for us through Christ. These good works are, however, helpful and are of benefit to God's creation and are therefore pleasing to Him when done in accordance with His will (see the discussion above on the Law and the two kinds of righteousness).

Sanctification, then, is the act of God in conforming us to the image of Christ (Romans 8:29). Through the process of sanctification, God takes those whom He has reconciled to Himself (i.e. justified) and works in them to make them more and more like Christ. As children of God, then, we are increasingly conformed to the image of God's only begotten Son, Jesus Christ. In this life, however, we will never be completely conformed; that is, we will not be perfect as Christ is perfect as long as we live in this fallen world.

The Latin phrase for this condition is *simul justus et peccator*, which simply means "simultaneously both saint and sinner." St. Paul speaks of this dual state of the Christian in Romans chapter 7, where he states that he finds himself at war with himself, doing the things he doesn't want to do while not doing the things he knows he should. We are all in a similar condition; we are justified by God and yet not completely sanctified in this life. Christians are not perfect, we still struggle with sin, even though we are justified in God's sight through Christ. We are both saints and sinners; saints because God has made us so through Christ, sinners because we are people who still sin and who live in this fallen, sinful world and await its full restoration. When Christ returns to restore his creation, then we will finally reach the state of full sanctification (1 Corinthians 15:49ff). We will no longer be plagued by sin, because sin and death and evil will be cast out of God's creation and we will live in perfect communion with Him and each other.

# 1 OUR TRIUNE GOD

## Guiding Passages

Isaiah 6:1-8

*In the year that King Uzziah died I saw the Lord sitting upon a throne, high and lifted up; and the train of his robe filled the temple. Above him stood the seraphim. Each had six wings: with two he covered his face, and with two he covered his feet, and with two he flew.*

*And one called to another and said:*

*"Holy, holy, holy is the LORD of hosts;*
*the whole earth is full of his glory!"*

*And the foundations of the thresholds shook at the voice of him who called, and the house was filled with smoke.*

*And I said: "Woe is me! For I am lost; for I am a man of unclean lips, and I dwell in the midst of a people of unclean lips; for my eyes have seen the King, the LORD of hosts!"*

*Then one of the seraphim flew to me, having in his hand a burning coal that he had taken with tongs from the altar. And he touched my mouth and said: "Behold, this has touched your lips; your guilt is taken away, and your sin atoned for."*

*And I heard the voice of the Lord saying, "Whom shall I send, and who will go for us?"*

*Then I said, "Here am I! Send me."*

Acts 2:14a, 22-36

*But Peter, standing with the eleven, lifted up his voice and addressed them...*

*"Men of Israel, hear these words: Jesus of Nazareth, a man attested to you by God with mighty works and wonders and signs that God did through*

*him in your midst, as you yourselves know - this Jesus, delivered up according to the definite plan and foreknowledge of God, you crucified and killed by the hands of lawless men. God raised him up, loosing the pangs of death, because it was not possible for him to be held by it.*

*For David says concerning him,*

*'I saw the Lord always before me, for he is at my right hand that I may not be shaken; therefore my heart was glad, and my tongue rejoiced; my flesh also will dwell in hope. For you will not abandon my soul to Hades, or let your Holy One see corruption. You have made known to me the paths of life; you will make me full of gladness with your presence.'*

*Brothers, I may say to you with confidence about the patriarch David that he both died and was buried, and his tomb is with us to this day. Being therefore a prophet, and knowing that God had sworn with an oath to him that he would set one of his descendants on his throne, he foresaw and spoke about the resurrection of the Christ, that he was not abandoned to Hades, nor did his flesh see corruption.*

*This Jesus God raised up, and of that we all are witnesses.*

*Being therefore exalted at the right hand of God, and having received from the Father the promise of the Holy Spirit, he has poured out this that you yourselves are seeing and hearing.*

*For David did not ascend into the heavens, but he himself says,*

*'The Lord said to my Lord, sit at my right hand, until I make your enemies your footstool.'*

*Let all the house of Israel therefore know for certain that God has made him both Lord and Christ, this Jesus whom you crucified."*

## John 3:1-18

*Now there was a man of the Pharisees named Nicodemus, a ruler of the Jews. This man came to Jesus by night and said to him, "Rabbi, we know that you are a teacher come from God, for no one can do these signs that you do unless God is with him."*

*Jesus answered him, "Truly, truly, I say to you, unless one is born again he cannot see the kingdom of God."*

*Nicodemus said to him, "How can a man be born when he is old? Can he enter a second time into his mother's womb and be born?"*

*Jesus answered, "Truly, truly, I say to you, unless one is born of water and the Spirit, he cannot enter the kingdom of God. That which is born of the flesh is flesh, and that which is born of the Spirit is spirit. Do not marvel that I said to you, 'You must be born again.' The wind blows where it wishes, and you hear its sound, but you do not know where it comes from or where it goes. So it is with everyone who is born of the Spirit."*

*Nicodemus said to him, "How can these things be?"*

*Jesus answered him, "Are you the teacher of Israel and yet you do not understand these things? Truly, truly, I say to you, we speak of what we know, and bear witness to what we have seen, but you do not receive our testimony. If I have told you earthly things and you do not believe, how can you believe if I tell you heavenly things? No one has ascended into heaven except he who descended from heaven, the Son of Man.*

*And as Moses lifted up the serpent in the wilderness, so must the Son of Man be lifted up, that whoever believes in him may have eternal life.*

*For God so loved the world, that he gave his only Son, that whoever believes in him should not perish but have eternal life.*

*For God did not send his Son into the world to condemn the world, but in order that the world might be saved through him. Whoever believes in him is not condemned, but whoever does not believe is condemned already, because he has not believed in the name of the only Son of God."*

## Our Triune God

The passage from Isaiah chapter six where the prophet is caught up before the throne of God is one of my favorite texts in the Bible. What many people may not realize is that the apostle John also referred to Isaiah's visions and prophecies. In chapter 12 of his Gospel, John says that although Jesus did many great signs before the Jews, "... they still did not believe in him, so that the word spoken by the prophet Isaiah might be fulfilled: 'Lord, who has believed what he heard from us, and to whom has the arm of the Lord been revealed?'" This statement refers back to Isaiah chapter 53, when Isaiah speaks of the suffering servant who would die for our sins, pointing to the coming of Jesus.

John continues, saying, "Therefore they could not believe. For again Isaiah said, 'He has blinded their eyes and hardened their heart, lest they see with their eyes, and understand with their heart, and turn, and I would heal them.'" This statement refers back to the words in Isaiah chapter six that come just after our "guiding passage" text.

Then, John gets to the clincher, writing: "Isaiah said these things because he saw his glory and spoke of him." This section of John's Gospel is speaking of Jesus Christ, and John says that Isaiah, in the Old Testament, wrote these things about Jesus because he saw Jesus and his glory. So, it is fruitful, then, to look at Isaiah chapter six more closely as this is the text to which John is referring, because in it Isaiah sees Jesus.

Isaiah was a prophet who lived in Judah in the 8th Century BC; his name means "Yahweh is salvation." He lived during the time period when the Assyrian empire had conquered the northern kingdom of Israel and were threatening the existence of the southern kingdom of Judah. The northern kingdom of Israel had abandoned worship of the Lord, Yahweh, and had gone after false gods, committing idolatry. The southern kingdom of Judah needed a prophet to call the people back to the Lord if they were not to suffer the same fate and fall to the Assyrians.

The beginning of Isaiah chapter six gives the time when Isaiah received the vision that he records. He says, "In the year that King Uzziah died I saw the Lord sitting upon a throne, high and lifted up; and the train of his robe filled the temple." Uzziah was king of Judah until his death in 740BC; this is when Isaiah saw this vision.

In the physical temple in Jerusalem, there were three sections. The innermost section was called the Most Holy Place, or Holy of Holies, because that's where the Ark of the Covenant was kept and where the glory of the Lord dwelt. Inside the Ark was where the two tablets of the Law were kept, and over the ark was a cover, called the mercy seat, where the Lord promised to dwell; shielding this mercy seat were two angels, called cherubim, with outstretched wings.

Now, way back in Genesis chapter three, when God expelled Adam and Eve from the Garden of Eden due to their sin, He placed cherubim in the Garden to "guard the way to the tree of life." These cherubim also acted as shields and prevented sinful humanity from entering into the presence of the holy Lord. So, on the Ark of the Covenant, we again see cherubim shielding the Lord's presence.

In addition, this section of the temple was veiled off from everyone but the High Priest. Only he could enter once a year into the Holy of Holies, on the Day of Atonement, and only with the blood of a sacrifice. Even the ground contained within the Holy of Holies was considered consecrated, and the chamber was filled with incense to veil the Ark from direct view.

However, in Isaiah chapter six the prophet sees not the Ark of the Covenant within the temple in Jerusalem, but the very throne of the Lord in heaven. He sees what the Ark and the temple in Jerusalem was only an earthly image of; Isaiah sees the heavenly temple to which these things pointed. And he sees the Lord whose glory and majesty is so great that the train of his royal robe fills the temple, just as incense filled the Holy of Holies in the earthly temple. Isaiah also doesn't see the cherubim, but instead sees a type of angel referred to as seraphim. He writes that above the Lord "... stood the seraphim. Each had six wings: with two he covered his face, and with two he covered his feet, and with two he flew."

The two cherubim on the Ark pointed to what these seraphim in heaven are doing, for they are also covering their eyes from the glory of the Lord. These seraphim seen by Isaiah cover their eyes with two wings, their feet with two more, and then fly with the other two. Thus, their feet do not touch the train of the robe of the Lord, nor do their eyes behold His glory. What was represented on the Ark and in the Holy of Holies is now seen by Isaiah in person in the heavenly temple.

As Isaiah is beholding all of this, one of the seraphim calls to another, saying, "Holy, holy, holy is Yahweh Sabaoth; the whole earth is full of his glory!" Yahweh Sabaoth is translated "Lord of hosts" in our Bibles. Yahweh is the personal name of God, meaning basically "He who is" or "He who causes to be." It is the name that He gives to Moses in the desert when Moses asks God His name (Exodus 3).

God calls Himself "I am," and gives Moses the name "He who is" (i.e. Yahweh) by which to call Him. Sabaoth means hosts, with the connotation of having supreme power and dominion. Thus, Isaiah sees the seraphim proclaiming the glory of the Almighty God, the Lord of hosts.

The word "seraphim" is only used a few times in the Old Testament. In Isaiah it refers to these heavenly beings who dwell in the very presence of the Lord and proclaim His glory. But, in the books of Numbers and Deuteronomy, it refers to serpents. The word "seraph" is the singular and means "burning one," which is probably how it came to be associated with snakes, due to the burning of their venom.

In Genesis chapter three, Satan is also called a serpent, but the word used there is different. The word is "nachash," which means "shining one." This usage reflects the fact that Satan is referred to elsewhere as a fallen angel of light. However, nachash is also used interchangeably with seraph to mean serpent.

In the book of Numbers the Lord tells Moses to make a seraph, a serpent, on a bronze pole to save those being bitten by venomous snakes; the text says that Moses made a nachash. So, the two words refer to the same thing, but looking at it from different angles. Notice that when it's associated with the Lord, it's a seraph, but when it's on the earth, it's a nachash.

In John's Gospel, Jesus refers to this event that is recorded in the book of Numbers. Jesus says, "No one has ascended into heaven except he who descended from heaven, the Son of Man. And as

Moses lifted up the serpent in the wilderness, so must the Son of Man be lifted up, that whoever believes in him may have eternal life."

In the book of Numbers, the people of Israel rebelled against God, so God sent serpents - the text says seraphim - which bit the people and caused them to die. But, whoever looked upon the serpent on the pole that Moses lifted up lived, even though he was bitten. Jesus, in John's Gospel, points to this event as foreshadowing what he would do on the cross. For through his death on the cross all who look upon him - all who have faith in the crucified Christ raised high up on the cross - will live and will be saved from eternal death.

Through the serpent Satan came sin in the beginning and death as a result of sin. And in Numbers we see the serpents biting the people to kill them, just as the serpent Satan brought death into the world in Genesis. But, through Christ being raised up on the cross, Christ is victorious over the serpent Satan, and over sin, and over death.

So, in Genesis Satan is referred to as a serpent and elsewhere as a fallen angel. In fact, in the book of Job, Satan is in the very presence of the Lord and accusing Job, and in the book of Zechariah Satan is again in the presence of the Lord accusing the high priest Joshua. He is the shining one. When he came to Eve to tempt her, he did so as one who appeared glorious. He wasn't all mangled like we imagine him; he tempted Eve because he looked like he was special. He was once an angel who was in the presence of the Lord, just as are the seraphim that Isaiah sees. But, Satan is now on earth, now just a venomous, slithery, death-causing nachash. It's similar to the relationship between seraphim and cherubim in the Bible. When the faithful angels are in heaven with the Lord, they're seraphim, but when they're on the earth performing God's will, they're called cherubim.

But, Satan is not faithful - he is arrogant and rebellious. The seraphim that Isaiah sees proclaim the Lord's glory and their singing shakes the very foundations of the Lord's temple; they are the heavenly versions of the faithful cherubim seen on the Ark and in the Garden of Eden. They burn and shine because they are in the Lord's presence and reflect His glory. Satan thought that he shined because of himself, he wanted to garner all glory for himself. This is what those who are rebellious against God do; they don't want to give God all glory. They become as a nachash - fallen, venomous, bringing death and condemned to death themselves.

However, the seraphim in Isaiah are faithful and declare the glory of the Lord. They not only shine, they burn with the reflected glory of the Lord. And Isaiah, as he encounters the holy Lord God feels his own sins. The faithful seraphim shield their eyes, but Isaiah beholds the glory of the Lord. So, as he encounters the holy Lord, he laments, "Woe is me! For I am lost; for I am a man of unclean lips, and I dwell in the midst of a people of unclean lips; for my eyes have seen the King, the Lord of hosts!" Isaiah sees Yahweh Sabaoth and knows that he will die, because sinful man can not dwell in the presence of the holy Lord and live. Isaiah has passed across the veil into the presence of the Lord and knows that he will die because of his sins.

But then, one of the burning ones - one of the seraphim - flies to Isaiah with a coal taken from the altar of sacrifice and touches Isaiah's lips with it, saying, "Behold, this has touched your lips; your guilt is taken away, and your sin atoned for." The Lord atones for Isaiah's sins through the altar of sacrifice. This is what Christ does for us. His cross - his altar of sacrifice - atones for our sins. Through the cross of Christ "... your guilt is taken away, and your sin atoned for."

And because the Lord Himself has atoned for our sins, we can stand in the presence of the Lord and we can also serve Him. We see this in Isaiah as the Lord, after atoning for Isaiah's sins, says, "Whom shall I send, and who will go for us?" Isaiah says, "Here am I! Send me." And the Lord commissions Isaiah to go proclaim His Word to His people. In the same way, since our sins have been atoned for through the cross of Christ, the Lord also sends us to proclaim His Word.

Thus, in Isaiah we see Law and Gospel - we also see justification and sanctification. We see the Law as Isaiah encounters the holy Lord God and feels his sins and experiences the condemnation for them. That is what happens to us as well when the Law works on us. The Law tells us that we are sinners. The Law shows us that we can not stand in the presence of the holy Lord God through our own efforts. The Law makes us exclaim, "Woe is me! I am lost!"

But, then we see the Gospel in Isaiah as the Lord atones for Isaiah's sins. We have this in the Gospel of Jesus Christ. The Lord does it all. So, the Lord justifies us and Isaiah in His sight by what He Himself does. The Lord justifies us through the sacrifice of Christ's body and blood on the altar of the cross. The Lord Himself enables us to enter into His presence and live through the actions of our ultimate High Priest, Jesus Christ, who entered into the presence of the Father on our behalf with the sacrifice of his blood on that ultimate day of atonement when he was crucified.

And then, we see sanctification - or the working of the Lord in us. The Lord sends Isaiah, because He has first justified Isaiah in His sight; likewise, He sends us, because He has first justified us. The holy Lord God justifies sinful humanity in His sight through His own actions, and then flowing from this freely-given justification comes sanctification. Our good works flow out of what God has first done for us, just as Isaiah's commission flows out of his first being justified by God.

We also see something else in Isaiah. The seraphim are calling out "Holy, holy, holy is the Lord of hosts" and Isaiah also hears the voice of the Lord saying - the verb is in the plural - "Whom shall I send, and who will go for us?" The seraphim have a threefold praise of the Lord - holy, holy, holy. And the one Lord God speaks in the plural, using both the words "I" and "us" to refer to Himself.

Holy, holy, holy - Father, Son, Holy Spirit. The Father is holy, the Son is holy, the Spirit is holy - one God in three persons. Isaiah beholds the glory of the Triune God and hears the seraphim proclaim the glory of the Triune God. He saw Jesus Christ there, because - as Peter says in the reading above from the book of Acts - Jesus is at the right hand of the Father and with the Holy Spirit.

In John's Gospel, as mentioned above, the apostle John says that in this vision Isaiah saw Jesus

Christ and his glory. John himself, though, also saw the glory of Jesus in heaven in the vision given to him that is recorded in the book of Revelation. It's called Revelation - not "Revelations" - because it is a single, consistent revelation of Jesus Christ given to John.

When John first saw the risen and exalted Lord Jesus Christ in Revelation, like Isaiah he also felt his sins in this encounter with the holy Lord. So, John fell at the feet of Jesus "as though dead," as it says in Revelation; the word used in the text means "corpse." John fell dead as a corpse at the feet of Jesus due to his glory. And like Isaiah, the Lord redeems John, placing his right hand upon him and saying, "Fear not, I am the first and the last, and the living one. I died, and behold I am alive forevermore and I have the keys of Death and Hades" (Revelation 1:17-18).

So, the Lord raises John up from the dead, because the Lord Jesus Christ himself died and now lives, having atoned for John's sin on the altar of sacrifice of the cross. And like in Isaiah, the Lord, having now raised John up, commissions him saying, "Write therefore the things that you have seen, those that are and those that are to take place after this." Jesus justifies John and then sanctifies him for the task at hand, just as he does for us.

Then, after Jesus gives John the seven letters to deliver to the churches, John is caught up in the Spirit to heaven and stands before the throne (see Revelation chapters four and five). There is One who is seated on the throne who shines radiantly with the beauty of jewels, and around the throne are 24 elders, clothed in white, with golden crowns on their heads. Thunder and lightening come from the throne, and before the throne are seven torches of fire, "which are the seven spirits of God," which represents the completeness and perfection of the Holy Spirit. Around the throne is a complete rainbow, connected end to end. It's perfect and circular, because God's promise of redemption is complete; He has delivered His people through the waters of Baptism in Christ, just as He once delivered the Church across the waters of the flood. And before the throne is a "sea of glass, like crystal."

John sees something else. He sees four living creatures with six wings who continually proclaim, "Holy, holy, holy, is the Lord God Almighty, who was and is and is to come!" Again, these creatures, the same as Isaiah saw, are proclaiming the threefold glory of the Triune God - the Father is holy, the Son is holy, the Spirit is holy.

John also writes, "And whenever the living creatures give glory and honor and thanks to him who is seated on the throne, who lives forever and ever, the twenty-four elders fall down before him who is seated on the throne and worship him who lives forever and ever. They cast their crowns before the throne, saying, 'Worthy are you, our Lord and God, to receive glory and honor and power, for you created all things, and by your will they existed and were created.'"

Since they continually do this, the Lord must be continually giving them back their crowns. The Lord has clothed the 24 elders with white robes, symbolizing Christ's righteousness with which He clothes them through the cross, and credits them with the crown of Christ's victory. Our Lord is truly gracious to us, to credit us with what He did for us through Christ. These elders that John sees are the twelve tribes of Israel and the twelve apostles; they represent the Church Israel of the Old and New Testaments, united in Christ. They proclaimed the Lord's glory and grace on earth and are now in heaven, continually proclaiming His glory and grace in eternity.

Then, John sees that the one seated on the throne has a scroll in His right hand, which "no one in heaven or on earth or under the earth" is able to open. And John weeps, because there is no one found worthy to open the scroll or to look upon it. But, one of the elders says to John, "Weep no more; behold the Lion of the tribe of Judah, the Root of David, has conquered, so that he can open the scroll and its seven seals." Then, between the throne and the four living creatures and among the elders, John sees "... a Lamb standing, as though it had been slain, with seven horns and with seven eyes, which are the seven spirits of God sent out into all the earth."

This Lamb sends the seven-fold, perfect Holy Spirit out into the earth so that the Spirit may testify to the Lamb. And the Lamb takes the scroll from the right hand of the One seated on the throne so that all things can be completed. And at this, the elders and the four living creatures fall down before the Lamb and offer up the prayers of the saints to Him. "And they sang a new song, saying, 'Worthy are you to take the scroll and to open its seals, for you were slain, and by your blood you ransomed people for God from every tribe and language and people and nation, and you have made them a kingdom and priests to our God, and they shall reign on the earth" (Revelation 5:9-10).

Then, joining the elders and the four living

creatures gather "many angels, numbering myriads of myriads and thousands of thousands, saying with a loud voice, 'Worthy is the Lamb who was slain, to receive power and wealth and wisdom and might and honor and glory and blessing!'" So, the angels come to proclaim the Lord's glory; for this Lamb who was slain - this Lion of the tribe of Judah who has conquered - is Jesus Christ.

John is in the presence of the Triune God in the heavenly throne room, with the Father, Son, and Holy Spirit. Then, John also hears "... every creature in heaven and on earth and under the earth and in the sea, and all that is in them, saying, 'To him who sits on the throne and to the Lamb be blessing and honor and glory forever and ever!'"

Many people do not realize what is happening here, but in this passage John sees a vision of the ascension of Jesus into heaven. In chapter one of the book of Acts the apostle Luke records the ascension of Jesus into heaven from the point of view of earth. Now, in Revelation John records the same event from the point of view of heaven. Jesus ascends back to where he came from, back into the presence of the Father and the Holy Spirit, back to where Isaiah saw him so long ago.

Thus, in this vision, John sees the elders of the Church proclaim the glory of Jesus Christ, he sees the four living creatures proclaim the glory of Christ, he sees the prayers of the saints proclaim the glory of Christ, he sees the angels proclaim the glory of Christ, and he even sees everything else in creation proclaim the glory of Christ. Heaven and earth are full of his glory!

The Holy Sprit testifies to Christ throughout all

the world, and the Father seated on the throne gives glory to Christ. Christ is the one who died and yet lives, atoned for our sins as the Lamb of God who takes away the sin of the world, and is the Lion of Judah who defeated sin, death, and Satan. In turn, Satan has been cast out of the presence of God and can no longer accuse us in His presence, because our Lord Jesus Christ has ascended back into heaven and has taken his rightful place at the right hand of the Father. Satan is no longer a seraphim, because he is no longer in the presence of the Lord, reflecting the Lord's glory. He is an impostor, a nachash, making himself out to be something he is not, bound to the earth and defeated due to the victory of Christ on his cross and empty tomb. All who try to take glory away from God for themselves are impostors, bringing only sin and death upon themselves and others who fall into their traps. However, because of the Lord's victory over sin, death, and the devil, the Lord clothes us with the white robes of his righteousness, so that like Isaiah and John we too will stand before His throne one day.

John saw this as well, writing, "... I looked, and behold, a great multitude that no one could number, from every nation, from all tribes and peoples and languages, standing before the throne and before the Lamb, clothed in white robes, with palm branches in their hands, and crying out with a loud voice, 'Salvation belongs to our God who sits on the throne, and to the Lamb!' And all the angels were standing around the throne and around the elders and the four living creatures, and they fell on their faces before the throne and worshiped God, saying, 'Amen! Blessing and glory and wisdom and thanksgiving and honor and power and might be to our God forever and ever! Amen'" (Revelation 7:12). All heaven and earth worship the Lord, because He made it, He redeemed it from the curse of sin and death, His glory fills all, and He defeated Satan and cast out his evil. The Lord is true and glorious.

One of the elders explained to John who this multitude is. He said, "These are the ones coming out of the great tribulation. They have washed their robes and made them white in the blood of the Lamb. Therefore they are before the throne of God, and serve him day and night in his temple; and he who sits on the throne will shelter them with his presence. They shall hunger no more, neither thirst anymore; the sun shall not strike them, nor any scorching heat. For the Lamb in the midst of the throne will be their shepherd, and he will guide them to springs of living water, and God will wipe away every tear from their eyes" (Revelation 7:14-17).

In the Old Testament temple in Jerusalem, the Holy of Holies where the Ark and the glory of the Lord dwelt was veiled off. No one could enter except the High Priest with the blood of the sacrifice. In Revelation, now here stands the great multitude of God's saints, whom Christ the ultimate High Priest has washed clean from our sins with his blood and made us priests, so that we may enter into the presence of the Lord. John sees us who have come out of the great tribulation of life on this earth to enter into eternal rest with the Lord.

Thus, no longer is there a separation between man and God, now the Lamb is in our midst as our Shepherd, feeding and watering us forever. We are all priests now, entering into the Lord's presence due to the blood of the Lamb - here in the Church through Word and Sacrament, and directly in eternity.

So, each week as the Church on earth celebrates the Lord's Supper (i.e. Holy Communion) and proclaims the Lord's glory and sings Hosannas to Christ in the company of the heavenly host, we join with all heaven and earth in proclaiming the glory of the Lord. We join in the song of the Church in heaven and the Church on earth, singing with one voice our praises to Him. And that great day of the Lord is coming when we will sing in the very, immediate presence of our Triune Lord God, just as John saw, shining in his presence, in the very presence of angels and archangels and all the company of heaven, proclaiming, "Holy, holy, holy, Lord God Almighty, heaven and earth are full of your glory!" Amen.

# 2 CREATION

## Guiding Passages

Genesis 9:8-17

*Then God said to Noah and to his sons with him, "Behold, I establish my covenant with you and your offspring after you, and with every living creature that is with you, the birds, the livestock, and every beast of the earth with you, as many as came out of the ark; it is for every beast of the earth. I establish my covenant with you, that never again shall all flesh be cut off by the waters of the flood, and never again shall there be a flood to destroy the earth."*

*And God said, "This is the sign of the covenant that I make between me and you and every living creature that is with you, for all future generations: I have set my bow in the cloud, and it shall be a sign of the covenant between me and the earth. When I bring clouds over the earth and the bow is seen in the clouds, I will remember my covenant that is between me and you and every living creature of all flesh. And the waters shall never again become a flood to destroy all flesh. When the bow is in the clouds, I will see it and remember the everlasting covenant between God and every living creature of all flesh that is on the earth."*

*God said to Noah, "This is the sign of the covenant that I have established between me and all flesh that is on the earth."*

Mark 6:45-56

*Immediately [Jesus] made his disciples get into the boat and go before him to the other side, to Bethsaida, while he dismissed the crowd. And after he had taken leave of them, he went up on the mountain to pray. And when evening came, the boat was out on the sea, and he was alone on the land.*

*And he saw that they were making headway painfully, for the wind was against them. And about the fourth watch of the night he came to them, walking on the sea. He meant to pass by them, but when they saw him walking on the sea they thought it was a ghost, and cried out, for they all saw him and were terrified.*

*But immediately he spoke to them and said, "Take heart; it is I. Do not be afraid." And he got into the boat with them, and the wind ceased. And they were utterly astounded, for they did not understand about the loaves, but their hearts were hardened.*

*When they had crossed over, they came to land at Gennesaret and moored to the shore. And when they got out of the boat, the people immediately recognized him and ran about the whole region and began to bring the sick people on their beds to wherever they heard he was. And wherever he came, in villages, cities, or countryside, they laid the sick in the marketplaces and implored him that they might touch even the fringe of his garment. And as many as touched it were made well.*

## Creation

Rainbows are fascinating in their beauty. A few years ago our family saw three rainbows at the same time down in Florida right after a rainstorm. We took a few pictures, but rainbows always look better in person. They are the bright, cheery light after the storm. Hurricanes may blow through, tornados may roar, and thunderstorms may clap, but at the end of all this violence, there is a rainbow.

In Genesis, God tells Noah that the rainbow is the sign of God's covenant. Now, to put this in context let's back up a little bit and review the familiar events of Genesis. When God created Adam and Eve, He created them and all creation good. Everything was perfect. But, Adam and Eve rebelled against God and brought sin and death into the world. Even in the midst of this rebellion, though, God promised a savior who would undue this rebellion and cast sin and death out of God's creation. And this promise was given to Adam and Eve, who formed the first Church, because they were people gathered by God around this promise. In the beginning the Church on earth was composed of just two people.

Then, Adam and Eve had two sons: Cain and Abel. Cain grew jealous of Abel, though, and killed him. Cain rebelled and separated himself from the promise; thus, Cain and his descendants were no longer part of the Church, because they lacked faith in God's promises and continued to rebel against God's will. Cain believed "in" God, so to speak, since he spoke with God; but, he lacked faith in God's promises that were centered in the promise of the coming savior, so he was not part of the Church. But, this wasn't the end of the Church or God's promises, for Adam and Eve had another son, Seth, through whom the promise and the Church would continue.

Thus, in the first few chapters of Genesis we see the line of Cain and the line of Seth diverging. Cain's line is rebellious, while Seth's line is faithful; it's the difference between the world and the Church. But then, as it says in Genesis chapter six, "the sons of God saw that the daughters of man were attractive. And they took as their wives any they chose" (Genesis 6:2). You may have heard or been told by others that this passage means that angels took human women as their wives; that's not what this passage means. It means that the "sons of God," the men of the Church of the line of Seth, took the "daughters of men," the women of the line of Cain - those outside the Church - as their wives, because they were attractive. So, they took as their wives any they chose, even those women who were outside the Church.

In fact, this happened again much later when

Israel went into Canaan, the promised land, after being delivered by God up out of Egypt. They, as the Church, were warned not to marry the women of the land who were outside the Church, because it would corrupt them. And the same thing happened again later when they returned to the land from captivity in Babylon. Likewise, St. Paul warns about this in 2 Corinthians 6, where he cautions the people of the Church not to be "unequally yoked with unbelievers."

That is good advice to young men and women. Do not be overwhelmed by someone's attractiveness, but rather focus first on whether or not someone is faithful, whether or not that other person you think is so cute is part of God's Church. It is easy to forget this when you're young, or think that it doesn't matter, but it should be the prime consideration. Ten/Twenty/thirty years from now, you'll be happier for it.

Just look at what happened in Genesis. The line of Seth began to intermarry with the line of Cain; those within God's Church married those outside God's Church. And the result was a corruption of those within the Church. When Paul talks about being "unequally yoked," this is what he means. When a believer and an unbeliever are married it is almost always the believer who is expected to compromise. Over time the believer will be pressured to give a little here, compromise a little there, until either their faith or their children's faith is overwhelmed and lost. The Church is always one generation from extinction.

I can't tell you how may people I've met who "used to go" to Church, or who "grew up Lutheran," who haven't darkened the door of a Church in years.

They and their children have become lost and tossed about by the spiritual and religious fads of our time. They are like sheep without a shepherd, torn at by wolves and, at times, becoming wolves themselves.

And this is what happened in Noah's time. After the people of the Church were corrupted, Genesis chapter six says:

"The LORD saw that the wickedness of man was great in the earth, and that every intention of the thoughts of his heart was only evil continually. And the LORD was sorry that he had made man on the earth, and it grieved him to his heart. So the LORD said, 'I will blot out man whom I have created from the face of the land, man and animals and creeping things and birds of the heavens, for I am sorry that I have made them.' But Noah found favor in the eyes of the LORD" (Genesis 6:5-8).

This is a hard text to read; God was sorry that He had ever made people, because of the evil in humanity's heart. Sometimes we all have times where we wish we hadn't been born; well, here's a time when God wished that we hadn't either. And this judgment against humanity's sin falls not only on humanity, but also on the rest of God's creation. Just as Adam and Eve's original sin in the Garden impacted all of creation, so too does this judgment in Genesis 6 fall on all creation. Humanity and this earth are intimately tied together, because we are both part of God's creation. The earth's wagon is hitched to humanity's horse, and God is the driver.

However, "Noah found favor in the eyes of the LORD." In our Bibles, the word LORD is in all capital letters. It is the stand-in English word for Yahweh, meaning "He Who is" or "He Who causes to be." When God appeared to Moses in the burning bush in the wilderness, He told Moses that His name is simply "I am." Only God "is;" everything else exists at His pleasure as His creation. Thus, God is "He who is" and "who causes to be" - Yahweh.

So, in Genesis 6, Yahweh - God - decides to save Noah and his family as well as the animals of the earth. God will save His creation from the waters of the coming flood through Noah. Noah is of the line of Seth - he and his family are part of the Church. In fact, they are the Church; only eight souls on the whole earth remain as the Church of the promise at that time. The Church had grown from the initial two - Adam and Eve - into a great many people, but then the Church compromised, was unfaithful to the Lord, and shrank down to only eight.

This should be a caution in our own time as we see Church membership dwindle in America. There was a time when America sent missionaries throughout the world to evangelize and spread the Church. Little did we know that the day would come when these nations would feel compelled to send missionaries back to America to evangelize us, because we have lost our way. The Church in Africa and Asia has grown and remained faithful to the Lord, while we in America have compromised.

We see denominations giving up on the Bible, treating it as if it is simply a book of history or ethics or, worse still, simply fables by which we soothe our troubled minds. We see Christians openly sanctioning sin, calling it "good" and "loving." We see humanity so turned in on itself that it no longer looks to God or to the wellbeing of the neighbor. We see humanity that seeks "only evil continually."

No wonder the church in America is shrinking; it's no different than the rest of the world. When we can no longer distinguish between Christians and non-Christians and between the Church and the world, because they have become so alike, then should we be surprised that people no longer see a point in Church and abandon it? When we lose our first love, Christ, should it be a shock that we lose everything else as well?

We wonder why our kids are killing each other in our streets, in our schools, in our theaters, and in our shopping centers. We want to find something to blame, so we blame guns, we blame movies, we blame video games; we blame everything and everyone but the one who actually deserves blame, ourselves. We in America have overwhelmingly neglected the Word of the Lord and discarded it as something that is irrelevant. However, it is supremely relevant; it's relevant because we are all sinners and are going to die, and only God's Word addresses this ultimate issue of humanity and gives us hope. It's not "guns," it's not "movies," it's not "video games" who are to blame - it's us and our sinful, rebellious nature.

And we see the end result of this rebelliousness and sin in Genesis when it grieves God so greatly that He decides to destroy everything. And yet, because of His Church, he saves His creation. Noah and his family are the reason we are here today, because they were faithful, they were the true Church. In addition, as mentioned previously, humanity's fate and the fate of the rest of creation are bound together; we see this in what happens next in Genesis. God has Noah build an ark on which to house samples of all the animals on the earth; everything that moves on the earth and that flies is taken into the ark, along with food to feed them all. The things that live in the waters will be ok and don't go into the ark.

In our children's Bibles and stories, the ark is normally pictured as some sort of cutesy, out of proportion boat. But, in actuality, it was a very large, very stable, barge-like ship with three stories. And in Genesis 6, God says to Noah, "I will bring a flood of waters upon the earth to destroy all flesh in which is the breath of life under heaven. Everything that is on the earth shall die. But I will establish my covenant with you, and you shall come into the ark, you, your sons, your wife, and your sons' wives with you" (Genesis 6:17-18). Then, God tells Noah to bring the animals onboard the ark that God will send to him. God Himself brings the animals to Noah to be saved on the ark, just as He Himself chose to save Noah and His family as an act of His grace and mercy.

So, the covenant that God makes with Noah is not only for Noah, it's for the animals too. The ark is the instrument through which God preserves His Church and His creation. The Church is a blessing to the rest of God's creation, because it possesses God's Word and promises. So, we mustn't let people try to tell us that Christians don't care about the environment; that's simply not true. God created His people to be His stewards and to tend to His creation. He calls us into vocation to serve His creation. And in Genesis 6, His Church preserved creation on the ark.

So, God has Noah and his family and the animals go onto the ark. And Genesis 7 says that "the Lord [Yahweh] shut him in." "He who is" - Yahweh - closed up the ark after Noah and everyone had entered into it. It's similar to how much later, Yahweh is the one who buries Moses in the desert after he dies (Deuteronomy 34:5-6). Yahweh - the Lord God - is always with His people, even in the midst of sin and death in the world.

After they entered the ark, it then rained for forty days and forty nights until the waters covered the entire earth and killed everything living on it. Out of all the living creatures and people that had dwelled on the surface of the earth, only those 8 souls on the ark and the animals aboard were saved. God's judgment of sin and evil is severe. And yet, He preserved a people for Himself and through them saved His creation, because He is also merciful and His steadfast love endures forever (cf. Psalm 136).

The flood waters covered the earth for 150 days until they subsided and Noah, his family, and the animals were able to come out of the ark onto dry land. It was like creation was beginning again; the old had been swept away in the waters of the flood and the new had been borne across the waters in the ark. St. Peter, in his first epistle, mentions Noah and the flood and the fact that they were brought safely across the water. He points out that Baptism corresponds to this, because in the waters of Baptism we too are brought out of sin and death and reborn anew as we are saved for the sake of God's grace through Christ (1 Peter 3:18-22).

After God delivers Noah and his family through the flood and into this newly reborn world, He commissions them in a similar manner as He had once commissioned Adam and Eve. He tells them to "be fruitful and multiply and fill the earth" (Genesis 9:1). Then, we arrive at our Old Testament text from

Genesis chapter nine where God establishes His covenant.

One important aspect of this covenant that we could easily miss is to whom God is making this covenant and promise. He is making it to Noah and his sons and their offspring that will come afterwards, meaning us. But, He's also making it with "every living creature." God's promise is for all people and for all creation; humanity and the rest of God's creation are intimately linked. And God promises that He will never again destroy the world with the waters of a flood.

God also gives a sign by which we may know that His promise is sure; He sets his bow in the clouds, the rainbow. We see it after rough storms and remember that God's promise of restoration and salvation is still with us and all creation. We also remember that God's restoration is not just for us, but for all creation as well, just as both Noah and his family as well as the animals were brought through the waters of the flood into a new world, and just as we are brought through the waters of Baptism into new life in Christ as we await his return to restore all things.

God says to Noah, "When I bring clouds over the earth and the bow is seen in the clouds, I will remember my covenant that is between me and you and every living creature of all flesh. And the waters shall never again become a flood to destroy all flesh. When the bow is in the clouds, I will see it and remember the everlasting covenant between God and every living creature of all flesh that is on the earth" (Genesis 9:14-16).

This is a pretty prominent sign that God gives

Noah. We see rainbows quite a bit in the sky after rainstorms. We see them with sprinklers in our yard or when we mist our gardens. The rainbow is everywhere. Oddly enough, though, it isn't mentioned in the Bible again until the end. It's only in the book of Revelation that the rainbow is again talked about. It's seen in Revelation chapter ten above the head of the mighty angel that straddles the land and the sea with his feet. The angel is wrapped in a cloud and surrounded by thunder. We see God's judgment on the earth coming with this angel, but we also see God's grace and mercy, because we see the rainbow.

And we also see the rainbow in Revelation chapter four. The apostle John is taken up into heaven in the vision he receives. As he stands before the throne of God he sees a rainbow around the throne, encircling the Lord. But, the word used for rainbow here and in Revelation 10 is different than the word used in Genesis. In Genesis, the rainbow is what we think of; a semicircular shape that connects two ends of the horizon. It's incomplete. It's not a full circle. It's the sign of a promise; a promise of restoration that is yet to be fully fulfilled and completed.

This is the sign we encounter in our lives. We live in the light of a promise of God, but we don't have the complete fulfillment of that promise. We encounter storms, we endure rough times, we suffer, we die. We still have the promise, though, but we haven't yet fully received it.

So, in Revelation 4 and 10, the word used for rainbow means that it is a full, complete circle, not like the rainbow mentioned in Genesis that is but a promise of the completeness that is yet to come. The rainbow is now full in Revelation, because all things are now complete. As the angels and the elders and the four living creations sing praises to the Lord, the rainbow is there, testifying to the completion of God's promises. He is no longer veiled by a cloud as He was in the Old Testament, but sits on a throne with a sea of glass before it, because now He has fully revealed Himself to His people through the one who was promised so long ago.

And then, John sees the one through whom these promises are fulfilled. In Revelation 5 he sees the "Lion of the tribe of Judah, the Root of David" who has conquered and fulfilled all things. He sees the Lamb who was slain and has risen who has come to take his seat at the right hand of the Father and who sends the Holy Spirit out into all the earth.

John sees Jesus Christ, because Jesus is the one who has died and now lives and who has conquered sin and death and Satan. He sees the Lord Jesus Christ who is the fulfillment of the promise of the rainbow; the one through whom the restoration of all creation comes thanks to his cross and empty tomb. The rainbow is complete, because Christ has fulfilled the everlasting covenant between God and all flesh that is on the earth. John in Revelation sees Yahweh in the flesh, but he's also seen him before.

You see, this is what is going on in the text from the Gospel of Mark. The disciples are on the boat, having trouble crossing the sea of Galilee because of the wind. And they think they see a ghost walking out on the water. They are terrified. But, Jesus "spoke to them and said, 'Take heart; it is I. Do not be afraid.'" The Greek expresses this more directly. What Jesus says to them is "Take heart; I am. Do not be afraid."

Jesus is walking on the water; he's not a ghost, he's the "I am," he is Yahweh in the flesh. He's the same God that Adam and Eve worshipped, the same God that Seth worshipped, the same God Noah worshipped and who shut Noah up in the ark, the same God Moses worshipped and who buried him, the same God the Israelites worshipped. But, now, here he is, in the flesh, fully revealed to us as Jesus Christ, the Son of God, Yahweh - He who is and who causes to be - in flesh and blood walking on the surface of the waters he created.

But, the disciples in the boat were astounded at all this, "for they did not understand about the loaves." Just prior to this, recorded in the preceding verses in the Gospel of Mark, Jesus had multiplied a few loaves of bread to feed a great crowd of people. But, the disciples didn't understand the significance of this. They thought it was a great miracle, but they didn't grasp the true significance. They didn't realize that they were in the presence of Yahweh.

The God who created Adam and Eve and all creation, and who spoke to Noah and to all the other prophets, had now arrived on the earth through His Son. This Yahweh is not only "He who is," but is also "He who causes to be." He caused all things to be in the beginning through His Word and now His Word is here in the flesh in Mark, causing bread "to be" in order to care for His people.

And now he is walking on water and calming the winds, because he is Lord over all creation and he has come to save and restore his creation. He can create, he can heal, he can call into existence things that are not, because He is the Lord God Almighty and his steadfast love endures forever.

And his steadfast love is for us, because He created us and saved us through his death and resurrection. God's covenant to Noah was a covenant made to us as well, and it is fulfilled in Jesus Christ so that we may dwell with Him forever, basking in the light of His glory and the warmth of his everlasting, steadfast love.

So, after the storms and thunders of this world cease raging, at Christ's return we will rise from our graves to gaze upon the great, perfect rainbow in the sky and upon the one who loved us so much that he died and rose for us and returned for us in the completion of God's promises. We will then disembark onto a new world, a world restored by God; His perfect creation. Amen.

# 3 MARRIAGE

## Guiding Passages

Genesis 2:18-25

*Then the LORD God said, "It is not good that the man should be alone; I will make him a helper fit for him."*

*So out of the ground the LORD God formed every beast of the field and every bird of the heavens and brought them to the man to see what he would call them. And whatever the man called every living creature, that was its name.*

*The man gave names to all livestock and to the birds of the heavens and to every beast of the field. But for Adam there was not found a helper fit for him.*

*So the LORD God caused a deep sleep to fall upon the man, and while he slept took one of his ribs and closed up its place with flesh. And the rib that the LORD God had taken from the man he made into a woman and brought her to the man.*

*Then the man said,*

*"This at last is bone of my bones
and flesh of my flesh;
she shall be called Woman,
because she was taken out of Man."*

*Therefore a man shall leave his father and his mother and hold fast to his wife, and they shall become one flesh. And the man and his wife were both naked and were not ashamed.*

Mark 10:2-16

*And Pharisees came up and in order to test him asked, "Is it lawful for a man to divorce his wife?"*

*He answered them, "What did Moses command you?"*

*They said, "Moses allowed a man to write a certificate of divorce and to send her away."*

*And Jesus said to them, "Because of your hardness of heart he wrote you this commandment. But from the beginning of creation, 'God made them male and female. Therefore a man shall leave his father and mother and hold fast to his wife, and they shall become one flesh.' So they are no longer two but one flesh. What therefore God has joined together, let not man separate."*

*And in the house the disciples asked him again about this matter. And he said to them, "Whoever divorces his wife and marries another commits adultery against her, and if she divorces her husband and marries another, she commits adultery."*

*And they were bringing children to him that he might touch them, and the disciples rebuked them. But when Jesus saw it, he was indignant and said to them, "Let the children come to me; do not hinder them, for to such belongs the kingdom of God. Truly, I say to you, whoever does not receive the kingdom of God like a child shall not enter it."*

*And he took them in his arms and blessed them, laying his hands on them.*

## Marriage

In the beginning when God created Adam, God saw that it was not good for man to be alone, so He created Eve as Adam's companion. Man and woman were created to join together in marriage to be one flesh, one body. They were created to correspond to one another and be each other's partners. And then they were commissioned to be fruitful and multiply. The marriage produced children as its fruit in order to populate and tend God's creation.

Adam and Eve were both naked, but were not ashamed. This was before their fall into sin, so there was no shame, no sin, no separation between Adam and Eve or between them and God. Adam and Eve were truly one flesh, and they were in perfect communion with their Lord. This is where chapter two of Genesis ends: man and woman as one flesh living in the presence of the holy Lord God. Everything was perfect.

However, they soon lost this perfection. We see it in the very next chapter, because Adam and Eve sinned and rebelled against God. This rebellion and sin brought separation not only between them and God, but between man and woman as well. The perfect marriage of Adam and Eve in the garden where they were so at one with one another, one flesh, was destroyed. The sin of Adam and Eve affected all creation, and it affected their marriage as well. They were now not wholly one flesh any longer and they were embarrassed to be naked, both before each other and before God.

So, the marriage of man and woman centered around the Lord was broken. The Lord had brought man and woman together, so He was the bind holding them together as one flesh. But, with sin came separation, and man and woman's relationship became strained, both between each other and between them and God. And this separation and sin continues to affect all human relationships in our own time, because things are not as they are meant to be.

So, sin intruded into creation and it encroached upon the relationship between man and woman and among all people. The interference of sin with marriage has continued to haunt marriages ever since. There's an international affairs writer named Robert Kaplan who makes the observation that you can tell a lot about a culture and society by the way it treats its women. In societies that put women down, objectivize them, or minimize their role, then you tend to see societies that are inward-looking and backward.

Robert Kaplan, perhaps inadvertently, hits on a Biblical truth. For God's purpose in creating Eve was not for Adam to have someone to serve and wait on him. He wasn't creating Eve as a pet or servant for Adam. No, the Lord was making a companion for Adam, and Adam and Eve were to be as one flesh. They were made to correspond to one another; that's what it means when the Lord said that He would make a helper fit for Adam. That phrase in the Hebrew means that the Lord was making someone to correspond to Adam, to be the right one for Adam, to be the only one that could complete Adam; and in turn Adam was the completion of Eve. So, Adam and Eve were created to be with each other, and man and woman ever since are created to be one with one another in marriage to correspond and complete each other.

However, in our sinful world we mess this up, just like we mess everything else up. Man and woman are tempted to use each other and to value each other only insofar as they are useful to each other. Sin continues to intrude into the marriage relationship. We see this in the text from Mark's Gospel as well.

The Pharisees come up to Jesus to test him with a question. They ask Jesus, "Is it lawful for a man to divorce his wife?" Notice that here, as in many places in the Gospels, Jesus answers a question that is meant to test him with another question. Jesus turns the tables on the Pharisees by asking them instead, "What did Moses command you?"

The Pharisees answered, "Moses allowed a man to write a certificate of divorce and to send her away." Wow, "send her away," that's pretty cold; it's like what you do when you're done with something that you no longer have any use for - you send it away to get it out of your sight. You go look for something else. It's the evidence of sin in this world that we send people away when they're no longer useful to us. So, when husbands and wives get tired of their partners, they can just send the other person away to make room for another person. It's like clearing your table at dinner, sending away the used dishes to make way for the next course. People are married for years or even decades and then one day decide that they want something new, so they send their spouse away.

And the Pharisees are people, just like us, and so they are not immune to this sin; they're sinners, just as we all are. And sending your wife away is a pretty harsh thing, especially in the ancient world. Sending a woman away was tantamount to plunging her into poverty and possibly death. Things were not meant to be this way.

And indeed, Jesus points this out. Moses didn't write this commandment because it was good or God-pleasing. No, "because of your hardness of heart he wrote you this commandment." So, the Pharisees thought that by writing a woman a certificate of divorce they were following God's Law and therefore without sin, but Jesus is saying that they are sinning, because this is not how things were meant to be. Divorce is a symptom of Adam and Eve's fall into sin. Their sin impacted all of creation and we see its effects constantly, and one of those effects is the divorce of married couples. It may be deemed necessary at times in our fallen world, but it's not God-pleasing, because God did not intend for this to occur. The sad, unfortunate, fact is that in our fallen world relationships are tainted with sin and sometimes marriages fall apart. But, this was not how it was meant to be.

Instead, as Jesus notes, in the beginning God made humanity male and female. Each one has its role to play and each one is incomplete without the other. And male and female are to join together in marriage to become one flesh. This is the will of God and the way He has made us. That's why from an early age we long for that which will correspond to us. And that's why it is so important to find the right partner and wait until the one we think we love truly does correspond to us. For, Jesus concludes by saying, "What therefore God has joined together, let not man separate."

Marriage was ordained by the Lord and is pleasing to Him, because through marriage His creatures are joined together as one. Marriage is so important to Him that it comes in the second chapter of Genesis. That is quite amazing and significant. The first chapter of Genesis records God's creation of all that exists, and then in the very next chapter He creates man and woman to be together; "What therefore God has joined together, let not man separate."

However, divorces do happen; marriages do fall apart, spouses do separate, people do send the one that corresponds to them away. These are all symptoms of our fallen world in which we live. But, this is not how God intends things to be. The

Pharisees thought that they were without sin as long as they gave their wives a proper certificate. Once they were done with their wives, they sent them away and no longer concerned themselves with them. Many husbands and wives in our own day do the same thing. But, this is not how things are meant to be. We and the Pharisees may do things perfectly legally, but it is still sinful and shameful.

So, what if we had a picture of how marriage was meant to be? What if we could see a model of the relationship that husband and wife are to have with each other?

Well, we have that picture with Christ and His Church. Throughout the Bible, the Lord often refers to Himself as the groom and the Church, Israel, as the Bride. And in Ephesians 5, Paul exhorts wives to submit themselves to their husbands as the Church submits to Christ. Lest we stop there and let sin turn our heads to think that this means that husbands are supposed to be cruel masters, Paul continues by exhorting husbands to love their wives as Christ loved the church and gave himself up for her.

Christ died for His Church to cleanse it and present it in righteousness before himself. So, the Church is the body of Christ, because she is his bride. And in marriage man and woman become one body as well, which is why it makes perfect, loving sense for each to love and submit to the other - because they're one body. They are one. Paul concludes by saying, "This mystery is profound, and I am saying that it refers to Christ and the church" (Ephesians 5:32).

But, this relationship that we as the Church have with Christ our husband is also tainted by our sin. In fact, in the Old Testament, when the people of Israel went after other gods and committed idolatry, the Lord charged them with committing adultery against Him. They were breaking the marriage relationship that they had with their husband. And in the New Testament, Jesus refers to the "adulterous and wicked generation" in which he lived, because people were not worshipping the true Lord God, but rather themselves and their own works, just like the Pharisees. They were breaking the marriage relationship by going after others.

However, the Lord is a faithful groom. Even when his bride, the Church, strays from Him, He never leaves. He is the perfect husband who always loves his wife. And the Church is called to be the wife who is always faithful to her husband. For through this marriage between Christ and His Church, new children of God are produced. Children of God are birthed through Word and Sacrament, Christ's gifts to the Church and his means through which the Church produces children.

So, the Church is composed of children of God. And we are called children for good reason. Children don't try to earn the favor of their father. They don't try to work for what they receive from their father. They simply receive their father's love and the gifts their father gives.

Likewise, the children of God receive all good things from our Heavenly Father by His grace for the sake of Christ. We are constantly in a position of receiving from God. We don't give Him anything He does not already have; just like when kids buy Christmas gifts for their parents, they're really spending their parents' money. So, we as part of the

Church are God's children who return to the Lord what he has first given us.

Now, at this point in the text from the Gospel of Mark, the disciples don't quite understand what it means to be the children of God yet. For when the people were bringing children to Jesus so that he may bless them, the disciples rebuked the people. They seem to be thinking, similar to the scribes and Pharisees, that Church is only for adults. They think, "You need to grow up a little before you can come to Jesus. You need to be old enough to be able to accept him. You need to bring him something for him to receive you."

But, these thoughts are all wrong, because the Church is composed of children born of water and the Word. The Lord births us as His children through the means of grace that He gives His Church. And so when Jesus saw that his disciples were trying to prevent the children from coming to him, he was angry and said to them, "Let the children come to me; do not hinder them, for to such belongs the kingdom of God. Truly, I say to you, whoever does not receive the kingdom of God like a child shall not enter it." And then Jesus took the children in his arms and blessed them.

What does it mean to receive the kingdom of God like a child? Children know how to receive gifts. They receive and are thankful. So, to receive the kingdom of God like a child means to receive God's grace and mercy through Christ as the gift that it is. We didn't earn it, we didn't deserve it, and yet God gave it to us anyway. We didn't do something to get our earthly parents to give birth to us, and we didn't do something to get our heavenly Father to birth us into new life through Christ. We deserve a lump of coal, but God gives us the free forgiveness of our sins and life everlasting and makes us His children through Christ.

So, as Christians, we are the children whom God has given Christ and birthed through His bride, the Church. We have been born of the water and the Word in Baptism. We are nourished with the body and blood of Christ in the Lord's Supper. We are fed with the proclaimed Word of the Gospel of Jesus Christ. Everything we have we received from God: our life, God's forgiveness of all our sins, and life everlasting. This is a gift.

So, we are not to despise the little children in the Church, because we are all as children before God. And we are also not to despise the bride of Christ, the Church, to whom we owe our births as children of God. We are all looking with yearning eyes to our heavenly Father for His gifts of grace and mercy through Christ. We are all like children, unable to offer anything to the Lord, but instead wholly reliant on Him. And this is a great relief and comfort, because the Lord is always faithful to His people. He is the husband who never leaves his bride, always faithful to His promises, and always bearing with the sins of His people.

Look at the Bible. In chapter one of Genesis, God creates the heavens and the earth. In chapter two He creates man and woman. Everything is perfect at the end of Chapter two. And then by the end of chapter three man and woman have brought sin and death into the world. If our salvation were up to us, we'd mess it up too. It only took Adam and Eve less than one chapter to mess up God's perfect creation. And then the whole rest of the Bible is the account of God's redemptive and restoring actions for His creation through His Son and his bride, the Church Israel.

So, our salvation depends entirely on Christ, and he has done this for us. It's done. It's already completely done. And that we can be sure of and rejoice in. He has brought us into the Church, birthed us as God's children, and loves and cherishes us as His own. All our sins are forgiven freely by God through Christ in this life, and when Christ returns for us, we will be perfected in the life to come as we and all the Church are presented in eternity before Him as a bride adorned for her husband. Amen.

# 4 GOD'S PROMISES

## Guiding Passages

2 Kings 2:1, 6-12

*Now when the LORD was about to take Elijah up to heaven by a whirlwind, Elijah and Elisha were on their way from Gilgal…*

*Then Elijah said to him, "Please stay here, for the LORD has sent me to the Jordan." But he said, "As the LORD lives, and as you yourself live, I will not leave you." So the two of them went on.*

*Fifty men of the sons of the prophets also went and stood at some distance from them, as they both were standing by the Jordan. Then Elijah took his cloak and rolled it up and struck the water, and the water was parted to the one side and to the other, till the two of them could go over on dry ground.*

*When they had crossed, Elijah said to Elisha, "Ask what I shall do for you, before I am taken from you."*

*And Elisha said, "Please let there be a double portion of your spirit on me." And he said, "You have asked a hard thing; yet, if you see me as I am being taken from you, it shall be so for you, but if you do not see me, it shall not be so."*

*And as they still went on and talked, behold, chariots of fire and horses of fire separated the two of them. And Elijah went up by a whirlwind into heaven.*

*And Elisha saw it and he cried, "My father, my father! The chariots of Israel and its horsemen!" And he saw him no more.*

Exodus 34:29-35

*When Moses came down from Mount Sinai, with the two tablets of the testimony in his hand as he came down from the mountain, Moses did not know that the skin of his face shone because he had been talking with God.*

*Aaron and all the people of Israel saw Moses, and behold, the skin of his face shone, and they were afraid to come near him. But Moses called to them, and Aaron and all the leaders of the congregation returned to him, and Moses talked with them.*

*Afterward all the people of Israel came near, and he commanded them all that the LORD had spoken with him in Mount Sinai. And when Moses had finished speaking with them, he put a veil over his face.*

*Whenever Moses went in before the LORD to speak with him, he would remove the veil, until he came out. And when he came out and told the people of Israel what he was commanded, the people of Israel would see the face of Moses, that the skin of Moses' face was shining. And Moses would put the veil over his face again, until he went in to speak with him.*

Mark 9:2-9

*And after six days Jesus took with him Peter and James and John, and led them up a high mountain by themselves. And he was transfigured before them, and his clothes became radiant, intensely white, as no one on earth could bleach them.*

*And there appeared to them Elijah with Moses, and they were talking with Jesus.*

*And Peter said to Jesus, "Rabbi, it is good that we are here. Let us make three tents, one for you and one for Moses and one for Elijah." For he did not know what to say, for they were terrified.*

*And a cloud overshadowed them, and a voice came out of the cloud, "This is my beloved Son; listen to him."*

*And suddenly, looking around, they no longer saw anyone with them but Jesus only.*

*And as they were coming down the mountain, he charged them to tell no one what they had seen, until the Son of Man had risen from the dead.*

## God's Promises

The Old Testament texts from 2 Kings and Exodus tell of Moses and Elijah. Moses came first. God used him to lead the Israelites up out of Egypt, then He gave Moses the two tablets of the Law on Mount Sinai. From merely being in the presence of the Lord, Moses' face would shine. His face reflected some of the glory of the light of the Lord. However, Moses veiled this shining light from the people, because they were afraid. Thus, they beheld the glory of the Lord as through a veil. Moses was the mediator for them before the Lord, and the glory of the Lord that he reflected was veiled from their sight.

Moses would be the mouth of the Lord to His people until his death. After the Israelites wandered in the deserts of Sinai for 40 years in punishment for their sin of rebellion against the Lord, the Lord finally brought them to the edge of the promised land. Moses would not be allowed to enter into the promised land across the Jordan river. He had brought the people as far as he could, but the Lord would use Joshua to bring the people across the waters into the promised land.

So, the Lord took Moses up to Mount Nebo, which is across the Jordan from Jericho. Moses was allowed to gaze across to the promised land, and then he died there. Deuteronomy 34 records all this and says that "... Moses the servant of the LORD died there in the land of Moab, according to the word of the LORD, and he buried him in the valley in the land of Moab opposite Beth-peor; but no one knows the place of his burial to this day. Moses was 120 years old when he died. His eye was undimmed, and his vigor unabated" (Deuteronomy 34:5-6). Despite Moses' great age he was still full of vigor and health, and yet he died. He had brought the people as far as He could with God's Law, but could not carry them across the Jordan to the promised land. So, the Lord himself buried Moses in the valley; the Lord took His servant and buried him in the ground to await the coming resurrection. Then Joshua succeeded Moses and led the people into the promised land.

At a much later time, Elijah was raised up by God as a prophet to His people. Elijah was sent to proclaim the Word of the Lord. His primary purpose was to call the people of Israel to repentance and back to the Lord. But, when his time was over, the Lord sent a chariot to take Elijah up into heaven. Then his mantle was given over to Elisha, who succeeded him as prophet.

This all brings us to the text from Mark's Gospel and the Mount of Transfiguration. Jesus takes Peter, James, and John up to a high mountain by themselves. It makes me think of the Lord leading Moses up to Mount Sinai. And when Jesus goes up on the mountain, "he was transfigured before them, and his clothes became radiant, intensely white, as no one on earth could bleach them." So, the disciples get a sense of what Moses saw on Mount Sinai. But, unlike Moses, Jesus' face doesn't just shine, all his clothing shines radiantly.

Then, the disciples also see something else just as amazing. They see Moses and Elijah with Jesus, talking with him. And we have to love Peter; he seems to speak when he's nervous. The text says that Peter is terrified, so he interrupts the conversation that Jesus, Moses, and Elijah are having to say:

"Rabbi, it is good that we are here. Let us make three tents, one for you and one for Moses and one for Elijah." Peter wants to keep them all here, because he sees the three of them - Jesus, Moses, and Elijah - as prophets. There was Moses first, then later Elijah, and now Jesus has come as another prophet; at least, this is what Peter seems to think. He wants to keep this mountain-top experience alive; he wants them all to dwell together in tents there.

But, then, "... a cloud overshadowed them, and a voice came out of the cloud, 'This is my beloved Son; listen to him.' And suddenly, looking around, they no longer saw anyone with them but Jesus only."

So, they hear the voice of the Father from heaven proclaiming that Jesus Christ is His Son and that they should listen to him. And then they saw no one, but Jesus only. Moses and Elijah have now gone, faded away, leaving Jesus only.

You see, Jesus is not just another prophet. He is not a prophet in the line from Moses and Elijah. He is the Son of God, to whom the prophets had been pointing. All the Law and the Prophets had pointed to this savior who was to come. And when Moses and Elijah beheld Jesus on this mountain, it was the fulfillment of all their hopes and dreams. They finally beheld - face to face - the one in whom they had hoped.

Moses represents the Law, given to God's people through Moses on Mount Sinai. The Law was not an end unto itself, though. As we see with the history of the people of Israel, the Law can only lead up to the borders of the promised land, it can not lead us into it. Only Joshua or Yeshua in Hebrew - known as Jesus in the Greek - can lead us across the waters into the promised land. The Law can not lead into the promised land, because the end of the Law is death, but the end of God's grace is life. And God's grace comes through Jesus only.

Elijah represents the Prophets, those who proclaimed God's Word to His people, calling them to repentance and pointing them to the savior who was to come. But, the prophets were not an end unto themselves, either. They did not point people to themselves, but used the Word of God to point to the one who was to come.

And now, here on the mount of transfiguration, this one who was to come has now come. He is the fulfillment of all the Law and the Prophets. He is the one to whom Moses and Elijah had been pointing and in whom all their hopes and desires lay. The Son of God has come, and God has decreed, "listen to him."

For Jesus is the one who leads into the promised land. He is the one who is the fulfillment of all of God's promises of salvation. And this promise was sealed with the death and resurrection of Jesus. For in his death and resurrection we have the confirmation that Jesus really is the Son of God and is the one, the only one, to whom the Law and the Prophets had been pointing.

Jesus has brought fulfillment to the Law and the Prophets. Moses died when his time was done, and Elijah was caught up into heaven when his time was done as well. Likewise, there is an finale to all the Law and the Prophets, and that finale is Jesus.

So, whenever someone tries to tell us that we need to do something to be saved, we ought to picture in our minds two things. The first is God burying the body of Moses in the desert, just as God buried the Law's accusations against us with the body of Christ. The second is God taking up Elijah the prophet when his time was done, just as God ended the prophets when the one to whom they had been pointing arrived.

And whenever someone tries to tell us that there is another way, or many ways, to God or that Jesus was just a great man or a prophet even, we ought to picture something else. We should picture Moses and Elijah - the Law and the Prophets - standing with Jesus on the mount of transfiguration. And then we see them fade away and Jesus only remaining with the Father from heaven saying, "This is my beloved Son; listen to him."

For it is only through Jesus that we are saved; he is not just a great man, he is not just a prophet, he is the very Son of God. He is God in the flesh, come in fulfillment of God's promises in all the Law and Prophets to save God's people. Jesus Christ came to save us. We are God's people; He has called us as His people as He has saved us through His Son.

"Jesus only." This is our watchword. This is our Gospel. This is our Good News. For all of our salvation depends on Jesus only. Who did anything for our salvation? Jesus only. Whose work merits our salvation? Jesus only. Who died for our sins? Jesus only. Who rose for our justification? Jesus only. Who reconciles us to God? Jesus only. In whom, then, do we trust to be saved? Jesus only.

If we try to add in our own works into the equation, we are trying to put Moses and Elijah back up on that mountain, because what we are really saying is it's not "Jesus only;" it's Jesus and something else. If we say, "Well, Jesus died for your sins, but you need to ...." Then it's no longer Jesus only. If we say, "Well, God wants us to do this or this to be saved," then it's no longer Jesus only.

We by nature are not "Jesus only" people. We are like Peter. We want to build tents for Moses, Elijah, and Jesus and treat them all as equals. We forget that the purpose of Moses and Elijah - that is, the purpose of all the Law and the Prophets - was to point to Jesus. When we have faith, then Jesus has arrived in our own lives and the Law is fulfilled and the Prophets are fulfilled, and they both fade away, leaving Jesus only.

We then have salvation with Jesus only, because we possess the treasure of God - His Word in the flesh. We possess Jesus only, and He is so loving and so wonderful that only Jesus is all we need. We don't need any works of our own to be saved, because we have Jesus only and His great work on the cross. We don't need any merits of our own, because we have Jesus only and His wonderful merit of resurrection from the empty tomb. Jesus only is all we need and we have him through faith.

This is why the rallying cry of the Reformation was grace alone, faith alone, Word alone. For it is through the Word that we are brought to faith in God's grace given to us through Jesus only. So, in the battle between sin, death, and the devil on one side and Jesus on the other, the victor is Jesus only. He won his victory on the cross and the empty tomb, and he gives us the benefits of this victory freely. So, we have all things through Jesus only who came in fulfillment of God's promises in the Law and Prophets. Amen.

# 5 FREE WILL AND GOD'S WILL

## Guiding Passages

Isaiah 64:1-9

*Oh that you would rend the heavens and come down, that the mountains might quake at your presence - as when fire kindles brushwood and the fire causes water to boil - to make your name known to your adversaries, and that the nations might tremble at your presence!*

*When you did awesome things that we did not look for, you came down, the mountains quaked at your presence. From of old no one has heard or perceived by the ear, no eye has seen a God besides you, who acts for those who wait for him.*

*You meet him who joyfully works righteousness, those who remember you in your ways. Behold, you were angry, and we sinned; in our sins we have been a long time, and shall we be saved?*

*We have all become like one who is unclean, and all our righteous deeds are like a polluted garment. We all fade like a leaf, and our iniquities, like the wind, take us away.*

*There is no one who calls upon your name, who rouses himself to take hold of you; for you have hidden your face from us, and have made us melt in the hand of our iniquities.*

*But now, O LORD, you are our Father; we are the clay, and you are our potter; we are all the work of your hand.*

*Be not so terribly angry, O LORD, and remember not iniquity forever. Behold, please look, we are all your people.*

Mark 13:24-37

*[Jesus said,] "But in those days, after that tribulation, the sun will be darkened, and the moon will not give its light, and the stars will be falling from heaven, and the powers in the heavens will be shaken.*

*And then they will see the Son of Man coming in clouds with great power and glory. And then he will send out the angels and gather his elect from the four winds, from the ends of the earth to the ends of heaven.*

*From the fig tree learn its lesson: as soon as its branch becomes tender and puts out its leaves, you know that summer is near. So also, when you see these things taking place, you know that he is near, at the very gates. Truly, I say to you, this generation will not pass away until all these things take place. Heaven and earth will pass away, but my words will not pass away.*

*But concerning that day or that hour, no one knows, not even the angels in heaven, nor the Son, but only the Father.*

*Be on guard, keep awake. For you do not know when the time will come. It is like a man going on a journey, when he leaves home and puts his servants in charge, each with his work, and commands the doorkeeper to stay awake.*

*Therefore stay awake—for you do not know when the master of the house will come, in the evening, or at midnight, or when the cock crows, or in the morning— lest he come suddenly and find you asleep. And what I say to you I say to all: Stay awake."*

## Free Will and God's Will

The season of Advent in the Church is traditionally a season of repentance in preparation for the Lord's return. We usually think of Advent as leading into Christmas and Christ's birth. This is certainly one aspect of Advent. This is the first Advent when Christ was born of the virgin Mary and God became flesh. But, then after his death and resurrection Christ ascended into heaven and took his seat at the right hand of the Father. He is still with us, though, through Word and Sacrament; this is often called the second Advent, because the Lord is still dwelling in our midst through these means of his grace. There is yet a greater day that is coming, though. On that day we will behold the Lord face to face. This is the third and final Advent when the Lord returns in glory for the resurrection and the judgment.

On that day, the Lord "will send out the angels and gather his elect from the four winds, from the ends of the earth to the ends of heaven;" Christ will gather his Church to Himself, all those who have died and all those still living. However, we do not know when this day will be; it is impossible for us to predict, because God does not give us the answer. So, Christ tells us to stay awake - remain faithful - and continue to look for his coming, because it will be at a day and hour we do not expect.

There is an important word in this text from Mark's Gospel that we may tend to gloss over without really registering what it means. The word is in verse 27: "elect." Christ says that his angels will gather his elect. What does elect mean?

Every year the President of the United States chooses a turkey to pardon for Thanksgiving. All the other turkeys continue to their deaths, but one turkey is chosen to be saved. One turkey is elected for salvation, redeemed from certain death.

Elect means chosen, more specifically, chosen by another. My analogy about the Thanksgiving turkey breaks down a little bit, in part because in the analogy the President is God and we are all a bunch of turkeys. But, the analogy is correct in the sense that we are all condemned already due to our sins, but God chooses us for salvation. He elects us; a fuller sense of the word "elect" that we often encounter in the Scriptures is "predestined."

I think that while we may be somewhat

comfortable with the words "elected" and "chosen," the word "predestined" causes us to become uncomfortable. The words "elected" and "chosen" leave us some room to equivocate and try to inject our own merits into the case. We may say, "Well God elected or chose us, because of something we did or something He knew in advance we would do; we gave God a reason to elect us, just as a politician gives voters a reason to elect him to office."

But, the word "predestined" closes these loopholes; for if something is predestined, then it is already decided beforehand. A political analogy would be that a Daley or one of his friends will be mayor of Chicago; it's predestined, it's going to happen.

However, this word "predestined" conjures up images in our minds of people who have no choice in the matter and have no free will. This is why it makes us uncomfortable. We want to hold onto our notions of "free will." This is where Lutherans come in with our "distinctions" for which we are sometimes derided, but these "distinctions" help us make sense of things.

One distinction is between the vertical relationship we have with God and the horizontal relationship we have in the world. So, in our horizontal relationships, or life in the world, we have free will, to the extent that any of us are truly free to do what we wish. We can choose who to marry, what car to drive, where to live, what size of peppermint mocha to drink. We have the ability to choose how we live out our lives in this world. But, this free will only applies to this horizontal realm of our lives in the world.

Where we mess up is when we try to apply this type of thinking to the vertical realm, our relationship with God. If we try to take the way things work in the horizontal realm - in the world - and force it upright to try to explain our relationship in the vertical realm - before God - then we end up on the wrong track. For if we believe we have free will with respect to our relationship with God, then we lead ourselves to believe that it is our choice to believe in God, that it is our choice to accept Christ, that it is our choice to be saved.

These are very common views, but also very dangerous ones, because they leave us on extremely weak ground. They put us on sandy ground that is easily washed away when the torrents of struggle and strife come. The ground is fragile, because it rests on us - the strength of our faith, the strength of our convictions, the strength of our "free will."

Eventually, the day will come when we will realize the truth of what the prophet Isaiah says when he wrote that "all our righteous deeds are like a polluted garment." Of all the things we do, of all the choices of "free will" that we make, our faith is the thing that we are most tempted to turn into our own work. In religion, our faith is the thing that we most want to hold up as the supreme example of our so-called "free will." We want faith to be our work, so that we can take credit for it.

Doing this makes our faith into our most righteous deed. And yet, notice what Isaiah says. He doesn't say that our sins or our bad deeds are like a polluted garment; he says that our "righteous deeds" are. Indeed, the word translated as "polluted garment" in this text has a strongly negative connotation; suffice it to say that Isaiah could not possibly have said it any stronger. So, if we try to maintain our sense of "free will" with respect to our relationship with God, we will reach the point where we realize that we are weak, our choices are weak, our convictions are weak, and our own "free will" may perhaps not be so free.

Over half of all marriages end in divorce. When all these people got married did they anticipate that they would get divorced some day? As they joined together in marriage and made their vows that only death would separate them from each other, did they ever think that maybe they wouldn't be able to keep these vows? Have you ever seen a wedding invitation that said, "Please join us as we celebrate the joining together of so-and-so and so-and-so in holy matrimony, for the period of 10 years," like it's a term life insurance policy? No, everyone when they get married pledges their undying love and fidelity to each other on the basis of their "free will." And yet, despite the strength of their convictions and the strength of their choice of "free will," over half of these couples will get divorced. So much for the strength of our promises.

If this is the strength of our convictions and free will with regards to things we actually do have some control over (i.e. our lives in this horizontal realm of life on earth), what does that say about our relationship with God (i.e. our standing in the vertical realm)?

I would submit that is shows the truth of what Isaiah says, that "... all our righteous deeds are like a polluted garment. We all fade like a leaf, and our iniquities, like the wind, take us away." Left to our own strength, our own convictions, and our own sense of "free will," we would forever remain lost and condemned sinners, because we will fail us and others. We have no free will with respect to our relationship to God, because we are by nature slaves of sin and condemned already. Jesus told Nicodemus in John chapter three that he came into the world not to condemn the world, because we are condemned already; he came to save us from this condemnation, because we do not have the ability or freedom to do so. We are by virtue of our fallen nature slaves of sin and death and can not free ourselves. All of our righteous deeds can not free us from this slavery, for even our righteous deeds are like a polluted garment.

Once we realize that we can do nothing to fix our relationship with God, a relationship that we broke due to our sinful nature and our sinful acts, then we are on the path to repentance. Once we realize that our faith is not our own work, then we are much better off. Once we realize that the Lord is our Father, that we are the clay and He is the potter, and that we are the work of His hands, then we begin to understand what grace means.

For grace means that God has elected us solely because of what Christ has done for us on the cross. Grace means that God has had mercy on us. Grace means that God has predestined us for salvation. Grace means that our salvation doesn't depend on the strength of our convictions, the strength of our choices, or the strength of our faithfulness, but on God's. Our convictions are weak, our choices are fickle, and we are unfaithful, but "God is faithful, by whom you were called into the fellowship of his Son, Jesus Christ our Lord" (1 Corinthians 1:9).

As St. Paul wrote to the Ephesians, grace means that God "predestined us for adoption through Jesus Christ, according to the purpose of his will..." and "[i]n him we have redemption through his blood, the forgiveness of our trespasses, according to the riches of his grace, which he lavished upon us... " (Ephesians 1:5).

Once our eyes are opened to this wonder of God's election, then we see it everywhere in Scripture. We see that God had favor on Abel's sacrifice, but not Cain's. We see that God chose Noah and his family to save through the waters of the flood. We see that God chose Abram as His own. And we see, as St. Paul wrote to the church in Rome, "... also when Rebecca had conceived children by one man, our forefather Isaac, though they were not yet born and had done nothing either good or bad—in order that God's purpose of election might continue, not because of works but because of his call - she was told, 'The older will serve the younger.' As it is written, 'Jacob I loved, but Esau I hated.' What shall we say then? Is there injustice on God's part? By no means! For he says to Moses, 'I will have mercy on whom I have mercy, and I will have compassion on whom I have compassion.' So then it depends not on human will or exertion, but on God, who has mercy" (Romans 9:10-16).

Our natural inclination is to recoil at the suggestion that God elects people for salvation, because we wonder about those who are not saved. Paul anticipated this objection to God's election, writing: "You will say to me then, 'Why does he still find fault? For who can resist his will?' But who are you, O man, to answer back to God? Will what is molded say to its molder, 'Why have you made me like this?'" (Romans 9:19-20).

So we see that our salvation is an act of God and done according to His will. He is the one who justifies us in His sight. He is the one who makes us right with Him. He is the one who brings us to faith through His Word. It is all His doing. The entire Scriptures reveal to us a holy God who justifies sinful humanity in His sight solely due to His grace which He bestows upon us through Christ.

However, we still wonder about those who are not saved. What about them? If God elects us for salvation, does He elect them for damnation? The answer is "no." For, Scripture says in 1 Timothy that God "... desires all people to be saved and to come to the knowledge of the truth. For there is one God, and there is one mediator between God and men, the man Christ Jesus, who gave himself as a ransom for all... " (1 Timothy 2:4-6).

So, we are left with a paradox that we can not solve, because Scripture doesn't solve it for us. On the one hand, we have the testimony of Scripture that God has elected us for salvation; He has predestined us for salvation even from the foundation of the world. And this isn't because He foresaw that we would do something to "earn" His forgiveness, for grace and mercy is a free gift given solely "according to the purpose of [God's] will" through Christ. So, He has chosen us as His own, even before we were born and apart from any works of our own, for even our righteous deeds are like a polluted garment and can not merit any reward from God. Therefore, the Scriptures testify that our gracious Father has had mercy and compassion on us through Christ, even before we existed. We also have the testimony of Scripture that God wants all people to be saved and that Christ died for the sins of all people.

However, we also know that not all people are saved, even though Christ died for their sins. The difference between those who are saved and those who are not is faith in Christ. This is a faith that trusts in Christ's death and resurrection for our salvation and thus puts on the righteousness of Christ as our own. But, even this faith is a work of God, for by ourselves we can not come to faith on our own power. For by nature we are slaves to sin, born into slavery due to the sin of Adam and Eve, and held captive and unable to free ourselves. But, God frees us from our slavery by creating faith in us through the working of His Holy Spirit in Word and Sacrament – His means of grace - when and where He pleases, "according to the purpose of His will" (Ephesians 1:5).

Therefore, we are left with an uncomfortable paradox that says the following:
- God is Almighty and in charge of all things
- God sent His Son Jesus Christ to die for the sins of all people
- It is our faith that grasps Christ's righteousness as our own
- Even our faith is a work of God
- God wants all people to be saved
- Not all people are saved

Thus, we are ultimately left with the following seemingly contradictory truths:
- God is all powerful and wants all people to be saved
- Not all people are saved

Why then, are not all people saved? The

unsatisfying, but thoroughly Christian answer is "we don't know." And we don't know the answer, because God doesn't give it to us, just as He doesn't tell us when the Last Day will be when Christ returns.

This is where Lutherans come in with yet another distinction. We make a distinction between what we call the "revealed God" and the "hidden God." The "revealed God" is God's will that we know through Christ; this is God's will that He has revealed to us that says that Christ died for all people and God wants all people to be saved. The "hidden God," though, is the hidden will of God; these are His actions and decisions that He does not reveal to us.

Therefore, the question of why not all people are saved belongs in the realm of the "hidden God," because God doesn't give us the answer in Scripture. What God does do, though, is call us to place our trust in what He has clearly revealed to us through the Scriptures and not try to delve into what He has kept hidden. This, then, is the "revealed God:" that Christ died for the sins of all people and God wants all people to be saved. Therefore, where God stops speaking, we do so as well. Any answer we try to give to questions not clearly answered in Scripture is pure speculation on our part, because God has not revealed the answer to us; some things He keeps to Himself and does not reveal to us for whatever reason that remains His own.

However, throughout history people have unwisely tried to answer this question about why some are not saved. One possible way to resolve the paradox is to say that God elects people to damnation. This seems logical. If God elects people to salvation, then wouldn't it stand to reason that he elects those not saved to damnation? This is the Calvinist view. But, the Scriptural answer is that this is not correct. God elects to salvation, but not to damnation, for He wants all people to be saved and come to a knowledge of the truth.

Another logical way to resolve the paradox is to say that it is something in the person that makes God save the person. Maybe it is their good works or their faith or their decision to follow Jesus? Many people hold to this type of view. But, again, the Scriptural answer is that this is not correct. Our faith and our salvation is entirely God's doing - we have no part in it.

So, what are we to do then? We are to subordinate our logic and reason beneath God's Word, the Scriptures, and content ourselves with what God has clearly revealed to us and not worry ourselves with what He has not revealed; for if He had wanted us to know His hidden will, He would have revealed it. But, instead, He chooses to keep some things hidden.

We are His children, and like children we only know our Father through what He has revealed to us. The Lord is our Heavenly Father, and we trust that He has revealed to us all that we need to know: that He created us, that Christ died for all people, and that He wants all people to be saved. The answers to some questions that trouble us are not for us to know, instead we are to trust in what we do know.

So, we are to "stay awake." We are to rejoice that God has had mercy on us, and we are to go out into the world to tell others of His mercy that He has had on them. For we can confidently tell people that

Christ died for their sins and that God has chosen them as His own, because this is what God tells us in the Scriptures. We know that Christ died for all people and that God wants all people to be saved through Him. This is the surety of the Gospel. This is why it is Good News; it is a sure promise because it rests on God who is faithful.

Thus, the answers to questions like why some people are saved and others not saved are not for us to know, because God doesn't give us the answer. The thought of election and predestination is uncomfortable for us, and it may cause us to wonder about how to tell if someone is elected or not (which is itself another thing that we need not worry about; let God worry about it). But, the doctrine of election and predestination is not meant to cause discomfort. Instead, it is meant to be comforting, because it shifts the focus from our works and our choices back to where the focus belongs: on God's works and His choices and what He tells us in the Scriptures.

Election and predestination are a comfort, because if we look at what God is actually saying in the Bible about election and predestination, He tells us that He has chosen us from eternity for salvation, that Christ died for the sins of all people, and that He wants all people to be saved and come to a knowledge of the truth. And so we can be sure that we are His people, because He has told us that we are. He has made this promise to us and even baptizes us with His Word and makes us His own. Whenever we begin to fear or doubt about our salvation, we remember that God's promise is for us and that He gave us this promise personally with His Word in the waters of Baptism.

So, in these last days before the final Advent, we are to stay awake, looking for the Lord's return, and going out into the world armed with His Gospel. We can boldly proclaim God's grace through Christ to all people, because God's grace is exactly that - His gift of mercy, and God has told us that His grace through Christ is for all people. And likewise, we can confidently know that we are God's people and that He has elected us for salvation, because our salvation rests on His Word and His Word says that we are saved. We also know that He chose us purely out of His grace and mercy on account of Jesus Christ's death and resurrection, not because we have done something to merit it.

It is a great comfort that our salvation doesn't depend on us. We are weak, we are inconsistent, we are inconstant, we are unfaithful. But, the Lord is strong, He is consistent, He is constant, and He is faithful. And He has promised us salvation and eternal life with Him through His Son, and He has gathered us together as His people in His Church, and He is returning for us on the Last Day to gather us together to be with Him for eternity. So we can be sure of this promise, because it rests in God and not in us, and God is able to fulfill this promise and is faithful to do it. So, until Jesus returns, we are to "stay awake" and wait for his coming, for we are His people for whom He is returning. Amen.

# 6 SUFFERING AND COMFORT

## Guiding Passages

Job 38:1-11

*Then the LORD answered Job out of the whirlwind and said:*

*"Who is this that darkens counsel by words without knowledge? Dress for action like a man; I will question you, and you make it known to me.*

*Where were you when I laid the foundation of the earth? Tell me, if you have understanding.*

*Who determined its measurements—surely you know! Or who stretched the line upon it? On what were its bases sunk, or who laid its cornerstone, when the morning stars sang together and all the sons of God shouted for joy?*

*Or who shut in the sea with doors when it burst out from the womb, when I made clouds its garment and thick darkness its swaddling band, and prescribed limits for it and set bars and doors, and said, 'Thus far shall you come, and no farther, and here shall your proud waves be stayed?'"*

2 Corinthians 6:2b-10

*Behold, now is the favorable time; behold, now is the day of salvation. We put no obstacle in anyone's way, so that no fault may be found with our ministry, but as servants of God we commend ourselves in every way: by great endurance, in afflictions, hardships, calamities, beatings, imprisonments, riots, labors, sleepless nights, hunger; by purity, knowledge, patience, kindness, the Holy Spirit, genuine love; by truthful speech, and the power of God; with the weapons of righteousness for the right hand and for the left; through honor and dishonor, through slander and praise.*

*We are treated as impostors, and yet are true; as unknown, and yet well known; as dying, and behold, we live; as punished, and yet not killed; as sorrowful, yet always rejoicing; as poor, yet making many rich; as having nothing, yet possessing everything.*

Mark 4:35-41

*On that day, when evening had come, [Jesus] said to them, "Let us go across to the other side."*

*And leaving the crowd, they took him with them in the boat, just as he was. And other boats were with him. And a great windstorm arose, and the waves were breaking into the boat, so that the boat was already filling.*

*But he was in the stern, asleep on the cushion. And they woke him and said to him, "Teacher, do you not care that we are perishing?"*

*And he awoke and rebuked the wind and said to the sea, "Peace! Be still!" And the wind ceased, and there was a great calm.*

*He said to them, "Why are you so afraid? Have you still no faith?"*

*And they were filled with great fear and said to one another, "Who then is this, that even wind and sea obey him?"*

## Suffering

I like the book of Job and tend to refer to it quite a bit, because what is in Job is instructive for us as we live out our lives in this fallen, sinful world, surrounded by decay, pain, suffering, and death. We see in Job what we see and experience in our own lives.

Now, Job is a good man. He worships the Lord and has faith. However, he undergoes immense suffering. First, he is tormented by the death of his children which pains him greatly and causes him enormous sorrow. And yet, even in the midst of this sorrow he says, "Naked I came from my mother's womb, and naked shall I return. The Lord gave, and the Lord has taken away; blessed by the name of the

Lord." What great faith that Job has in the Lord. Even when things are horrible, he still trusts in the Lord; blessed be the name of the Lord.

After losing his children, Job is then plagued by sores and bad health, and in his suffering his wife comes to him and says, "Do you still hold fast your integrity? Curse God and die." She thinks that since Job is suffering so greatly obviously God has deserted him. However, Job replies to her, "Shall we receive good from God, and shall we not receive evil?" Job is still trusting in the Lord, despite all that he is suffering.

Then, his three friends come to visit him. They are named Eliphaz, Bildad, and Zophar. The text says that they came to show Job sympathy and comfort him. They sat in silence with him for seven days without saying anything, because they saw that he was suffering greatly. Then, finally, Job spoke and cursed the day of his birth. The suffering finally got to him. His family was gone, he was suffering ill health, and nothing seemed to be going right. He wished that he had never been born. Haven't we all had days like this as well? Haven't we often looked for answers for our sorrows too?

In response to Job's cries, his friend Eliphaz is the first to offer his opinion to Job to try to comfort him. He explains to Job that God punishes those who do evil and saves those who do good. He tells Job that although bad things are happening to him, good will come from it if he only grasps hold of the Lord.

Then, Bildad offers his opinion. His argument is similar to Eliphaz's; he says that if Job will seek God to plead with Him for mercy and if he is pure and upright, then God will make everything better and all will turn out for the best.

Then, Zophar gives his advice. His is similar to the advice of the other two friends. He says that God punishes evil and that Job must have done something bad to be punished by God. He needs to figure out what he did wrong and make it right.

Eliphaz, Bildad, and Zophar had come to Job to offer him sympathy and comfort. But, what they say to him as he mourns the loss of his children, endures the scorn of his wife, and suffers with sores from head to toe is anything but comforting. His friends are telling him variations of things like: God is punishing you for some sin you've committed, but things will get better and everything will turn out for the best. Is this a comfort for Job? Would it be a comfort for us?

I don't think so. In fact, Job isn't comforted by his friends. He says, "... how can a man be in the right before God? ... Who will say to him, 'What are you doing?'" He recognizes that none of us have a claim to God's favor. We always rely on His grace.

Then, Job brings his complaint directly to God, saying to Him, "Does it seem good to you to oppress, to despise the work of your hands and favor the designs of the wicked?" Job wants to know why God is allowing this to happen. Job wants to know why bad things happen to good people and why good things happen to bad people. Why is he suffering? Does God not care that he is perishing? Aren't these questions that we also have at times?

In response, another man named Elihu, who had been listening the whole time to the debate among Job and his friends, offers his opinion. The text says that Elihu burned with anger at Job, because Job justified himself rather than God, and that he also burned with anger at Job's three friends, "because they had found no answer, although they had declared Job to be in the wrong." So, Elihu wants to justify God and find an answer, a reason that is, for Job's suffering. He is younger than the other men, but claims to have wisdom from the Spirit of God and therefore to be speaking for God.

So, Elihu wants to justify God's actions. He says, "... far be it from God that he should do wickedness, and from the Almighty that he should do wrong. For according to the work of a man he will replay him, and according to his ways he will make it befall him" (Job 34:10-11). Basically, he is saying that Job must have done something wrong to merit the sufferings he is undergoing. He also argues that God sends trials upon a person to strengthen that person and bring him back to the Lord. So, Elihu claims to be speaking on God's behalf and wants to justify God's actions so that God appears in the right (Job 36:2).

Now, I don't really find Elihu's argument any more comforting than the arguments of Job's three friends. Elihu is still basically telling Job that either he did something wrong for which God is punishing him, or that God is strengthening him through these trials. We hear people say similar things in our own day. When something bad happens to a person, otherwise well-meaning people try to offer a reason for why that happened. They mean well, just like Job's friends and Elihu mean well. They say things like, "Well, it happened for a reason" or "God will bring good from this" or "You're better off anyway" or "It happens to everyone" or "God only gives you what He knows you can handle" or even sometimes "You must have done something wrong."

These are the types of things that Job's friends and Elihu tell him. In the first 37 chapters of the book of Job they try to explain to Job why he is undergoing suffering. And in all of these chapters with all of their great many words all of their answers fall short. Not one of them is helpful and comforting and sympathetic to Job. They have failed in their desire to offer Job sympathy and comfort. However, most importantly, not one of them thought to lodge a complaint directly with God, except for Job himself. The others talked "about" God, but Job talked "to" God, bringing his complaint before the Lord.

So, then, in chapter 38 the Lord finally speaks. Right after Elihu, who claimed to be speaking for the Lord, finishes speaking the Lord Himself says, "Who is this that darkens counsel by words without knowledge? Dress for action like a man; I will question you, and you make it known to me." God basically says, "If these people are so smart, then surely they must have been there when God created all things. They must know everything!"

But, they don't. In all of their words that they gave to Job, and in all of Elihu's words where he claimed to be speaking on behalf of God, not one of those words came from God Himself. They were speaking things that the Lord Himself had not revealed to them. They spoke where God had not spoken.

That's the problem, really, with all of these explanations. Not one of them comes from God. God doesn't really tell Job and his friends why Job is suffering. There is no real explanation; Job's friends are just speculating at the reason. And God doesn't tell us why we suffer in this life. There is no real explanation given to us. When we try to explain why, beyond stating that we live in a fallen world with sin and death, then we speak where God has not spoken; we are just speculating. We get caught in the trap of trying to explain what we see in terms of God's hidden will.

There are some things we know about God and some things we don't know. Everything we know is what He Himself reveals to us. Everything else is hidden from us, and we - in our fallen, fallible, human reasoning - can not discover what God chooses to keep hidden. So, we can not explain what God has not told us. We don't have a real answer to why we suffer.

But, the fact that there is no explanation for why we suffer in life isn't a very satisfying answer, is it? We want to know why. We offer up our own opinions as to why, and other people offer their opinions too. However, these opinions come from words without knowledge. They come from fallen human reasoning. They may even come from a pious yearning to justify God; the desire to justify God's actions so that He appears in a positive light.

This act of speaking where God has not spoken leads to some perverse logic. When the September 11th attacks on America occurred, people tried to explain it in terms of God's will. Perhaps God was punishing the United States? Perhaps God couldn't stop it? Perhaps God didn't know about it? When something tragic happens people want to try to explain it. But when we do, our answers fall short.

There are three fundamental things that we believe about God. We believe that He is all powerful; we believe that He is all knowing; and we believe that He is good. How, then, do we explain the presence of evil in the world? How do we explain why bad things happen to good people and why good things happen to evil people?

When we try to answer these questions, what we're essentially doing is trying to justify God. The theological term for this is "theodicy;" that just means trying to make excuses for God. We're trying to say how He is all powerful, how He is all knowing, and how He is good, even when things in the world don't seem to show this. We want to answer for God's actions so that He doesn't appear in a bad light.

However, God needs no justification. He created the world; He is Lord over creation. We make a distinction between what God reveals to us and what He keeps hidden. This is the distinction between His "revealed will" and His "hidden will." What is hidden is why there is still evil and suffering in this world and why good people suffer. Why did September 11th happen? Why did Hurricane Katrina hit New Orleans? Why did the Tsunami hit Indonesia? Why do children die? Why are there predators, abusers, and murderers in the world? The answer that does not satisfy us is that we ultimately don't know. God doesn't tell us why, so we are not to speak for Him where He has not spoken.

This causes us to recoil and cry out to Him in pain and anguish and even anger, "Do you not care that we are perishing?" The disciples did this in the Gospel text from Mark. They're in a boat on the Sea of Galilee, which is a very large lake that gets hit by sudden storms.  So, they're on this boat when a storm comes.  The waves were breaking into the boat, and it was filling with water.  And there's Jesus.  And what is he doing?  He's sleeping.  He seems not to care.  Doesn't God care?  Isn't He awake?  The boat is going to sink, and he isn't even going to do anything about it.

Thus, the disciples wake Jesus up and say, "Teacher, do you not care that we are perishing?"  So, Jesus woke up "... and rebuked the wind and said to the sea, 'Peace!  Be still!'  And the wind ceased, and there was a great calm."  Then, Jesus turned to the disciples and said, "Why are you so afraid?  Have you still no faith?"  And the disciples "... were filled with great fear and said to one another, 'Who then is this, that even wind and sea obey him?'"

The cry of the disciples is the same as the cry of Job.  Doesn't God care?  In the answer that God gives Job, God says that it is He who says to the sea, "Thus far shall you come, and no farther, and here shall your proud waves be stayed?"  And in Mark's Gospel we see exactly this.  Jesus stays the waves and rebukes the wind and brings everything back under control.  Even the wind and sea obey him, because he is Lord over creation.  He is the incarnate Word of God through whom the Father spoke all things into existence.  He is the strong Word made flesh.

Jesus Christ is the one through whom God is restoring creation.  We live in a fallen world, a world with sin and death and evil.  But, this is not how God created the world.  He created it good and perfect, but humanity fell into sin and brought death and evil into God's creation.

Thus, we're living in this post-fall world,

experiencing the effects of the fall, living in the midst of trials and tribulations. So, we cry out to God, "Do you not care that we are perishing?" Where was God on September 11th? Where was God during Hurricane Katrina? Where was God during the great tsunami? Where was God in all the pain and anguish in the world? Where is God in my own life as I'm suffering?

The fact is that God is on the cross, dying for us, suffering with us; our Redeemer came down to us. We meet the revealed God under the shadow of the cross as God in the flesh dies on it for us. We don't have the answers to why bad things happen to good people, we don't have answers for why God allows evil to persist in this world, but what we do know is the same thing that Job knew, because God reveals it to us: "I know that my Redeemer lives, and at the last he will stand upon the earth. And after my skin has been thus destroyed, yet in my flesh I shall see God, whom I shall see for myself, and my eyes shall behold, and not another" (Job 19:25-27).

We know God's grace and mercy and love through Jesus Christ. We grasp hold of this comfort as we endure trials and sufferings in this life and face pain for which we don't have the answers. We look to the cross of Christ, because this Jesus Christ even the wind and sea obey. He is coming again to restore all creation. The God who created all things is returning to restore all things through His strong Word.

So, we walk by faith and not by sight. We see evil, we see pain, we see suffering. But, what we trust in is what we don't see. We trust that the Lord who created all things has not abandoned us. We trust that He does care that we are perishing. And we trust that He will not abandon us to the grave, but will return for us. This Lord over creation, the Word whom even the wind and sea obey, will return to restore His creation.

When Christ our Lord returns there will no longer be pain and suffering and evil. He will cast these out, even as he rebukes the wind and sea; all things will be restored. We will see our Redeemer face to face on that day, as he returns for us.

In this life we don't have all the answers. When something bad happens to us or to someone else, we ultimately don't have the answer for why it happened. The most we can say is, "That's horrible, I'm sorry." But, there's one more thing we can say and know; we know that our Redeemer lives. He who died and rose again is returning for us. So, our hopes are focused out on the horizon as we look for Christ's return. The Lord does care that we are perishing, that is why He is returning to make all things right and to fix His creation so that we may live in peace with Him and each other forever. Amen.

# 7 BROKENNESS AND RESTORATION

## Guiding Passages

Ecclesiastes 12:13-14

*The end of the matter; all has been heard. Fear God and keep his commandments, for this is the whole duty of man. For God will bring every deed into judgment, with every secret thing, whether good or evil.*

Matthew 11:12-19

*[Jesus said,] "From the days of John the Baptist until now the kingdom of heaven has suffered violence, and the violent take it by force. For all the Prophets and the Law prophesied until John, and if you are willing to accept it, he is Elijah who is to come. He who has ears to hear, let him hear.*

*But to what shall I compare this generation? It is like children sitting in the marketplaces and calling to their playmates,*

*'We played the flute for you, and you did not dance;
we sang a dirge, and you did not mourn.'*

*For John came neither eating nor drinking, and they say, 'He has a demon.' The Son of Man came eating and drinking, and they say, 'Look at him! A glutton and a drunkard, a friend of tax collectors and sinners!' Yet wisdom is justified by her deeds."*

## Brokenness and Restoration

The writer of the Old Testament book of Ecclesiastes struggled with the meaning of life. He sought meaning in wisdom, power, wealth, and pleasure; and yet, he saw that all these things will pass away. He also saw that there is much injustice and evil in the world. He saw that all people will one day return to the dust from which we were originally created. The writer was wise, strong, wealthy, and enjoyed a world of pleasures. And yet, in none of these things did he find true meaning or happiness.

It is the same with us today. We often feel a void in our lives, and we know that we need to fill it with something. Some people spend their entire lives searching for meaning, just like the writer of Ecclesiastes. People try to fill the void with money, with possessions, with other people, and with pleasure. People look to creation to fulfill their needs, rather than to the Creator. However, creation will always leave us wanting more, because it can not fill the void that only God can fill. Only the Creator can fix the hurt, brokenness, and longing that we have.

The writer of Ecclesiastes eventually realized this too. For after considering all other possible sources of meaning - things like wisdom, power, wealth and pleasure - this was his conclusion:

"The end of the matter; all has been heard. Fear God and keep his commandments, for this is the whole duty of man. For God will bring every deed into judgment, with every secret thing, whether good or evil" (Ecclesiastes 12:13-14).

"Fear God and keep his commandments," this is what God created us to do. In the beginning, He created Adam and Eve to be His people with whom He could dwell. The Creator would live in the midst of His creatures in the midst of His creation. And as their Creator, He expected them to look to Him - and only Him - for all things and to obey His holy will - they were to "fear God and keep his commandments."

God expects this because He is our Creator and

everything comes from Him. What is more, He is gracious to give to us freely; He does not charge us for the air we breathe, the food we eat, or the very life we live. So, as our Creator, we are to look to Him for all good things and to have Him only as our God; this is what it means to fear God, we look to Him as our one and only God. This is what He created us to do - "fear God and keep his commandments" - and in doing so we exercise our full humanity. For humanity was created to know God and obey His will. This was the original state of humanity; perfect humanity in perfect communion with God and with each other.

However, Adam and Eve soon rebelled against God. They lost their fear of Him and so disobeyed His will; they looked somewhere else for good and trusted in something else. Their first sin was to break the First Commandment - for they committed idolatry by putting something else in the spot only the Lord should occupy - and this led to the breaking of all the other commandments and a whole host of sins.

Thus, when we misuse the Lord's name, neglect His Word and worship, disobey our parents and civil authority, hate and kill, cheat on our spouses, lie and spread rumors, steal, and covet the possessions of others, we do these things because we have neglected to "fear God." We are natural born idolaters who constantly fail to have the Lord as our only God; we tend to look to other things for comfort and good - we trust in our wealth, our pleasures, our knowledge, or our power. And by trusting in these things, we make these things into our gods, idols who can not give life, but only lead to an unfulfilled void and, ultimately, death.

Thus, due to the sin of Adam and Eve, like

them we too have lost part of our humanity; we can no longer perfectly "fear God and keep his commandments." We are less than God created us to be. We are born into sin, into a state of rebellion against God. We are broken and so we can not by nature "fear God and keep His commandments," because we are - due to our broken, fallen nature - His enemies.

This is not, though, how God created us to be; He created us to be in perfect communion with Him and with each other. Due to the sin of Adam and Eve, though, this perfection is now broken - we are fallen. And so we have lost part of our humanity - we have fallen away from the origin, away from God, away from our Creator. And so we are lost and condemned creatures from the moment we come into the world, for the "wages of sin is death" (Romans 6:23). We are natural born sinners who face an eternal death separated from God for eternity - forever estranged from our Creator, our Heavenly Father. How awful this condemnation is, to never be with our Father again. We are, due to our fallen nature, truly slaves to sin. We can not free ourselves.

This is not, though, how God intended it to be, and there is one who can and does set us free. Our Heavenly Father sent His Son to us to free us. God came down to us, in the flesh, into His creation to free us from our sins. We can not free ourselves through our own power, because we can not be perfect. We can not "fear God and keep his commandments" perfectly, because we are born in sin. We are tainted; so, despite our best efforts we can not purge all sin from ourselves, and we can not make ourselves right before God.

But, the Son can, and does, free us. Jesus Christ can "fear God and keep his commandments," because he is perfect. He is the perfect man, truly fully human because he is sinless; he is unbroken and unfallen. He is also the perfect God, truly fully God, existing from eternity in unity with the Father and the Holy Spirit. So, in him, God has reconciled humanity with God. God has reconciled us to Himself in the person of Jesus Christ, uniting his humanity with his deity in perfect communion, just as he now unites us with him. The Son did what we could not: "fear God and keep his commandments." And the Father credits us with this work of His Son that he did on our behalf.

But what of our failure to do God's will? What of our punishment that we deserve? Jesus Christ bore that for us. God poured out His wrath on His Son. Christ took upon Himself the punishment for our sins and died on the cross and rose on the third day. And He did this to bring us back to Him. Since we could not repay God for our sins and we could not bear the burden of His punishment, His Son made the payment for us and bore the punishment we deserve.

Thus, God has reconciled us back to God. The Son has brought us back to the Father. God has done it all. He has accomplished all of our salvation. Christ died and rose so that we too will rise, although we die. And so, the entire initiative and work of our salvation rests with God. He has done it all, and what a wonderful gift that is!

But we, being the sinful humans that we are, are constantly tempted to try to take credit for our salvation. We want to have some part in it and be able to glory in our own works. We want to throw up our own perceived "goodness" in front of God. We want to force our way into heaven through the apparent strength of our own works, our own merits, and our own strivings. The kingdom of heaven suffers violence, and the violent take it by force - we want to use the power of our own works and merits to force our way into heaven. We want it to be about what we're doing - "it's our right to be in heaven - we're good people," we say.

However, we are warned, "Fear God and give him glory, because the hour of his judgment has come, and worship him who made heaven and earth, the sea and the springs of water" (Revelation 14:7). For only to God belongs the glory for our salvation, and only Him are we to fear as our God. He has done it all for us. Just as He created us and all things, so too is He recreating us and all things through Christ.

We see the beginning of this recreation and restoration in Christ's Church as God has birthed the people of his Church as new creations in Christ through the waters of Baptism. And not only is God restoring His people through Christ; He is also restoring the entire fallen creation to Himself through Christ. For "heaven" where we will live forever is not some cloud bank populated by a bunch of harpists; rather, it is God's restored creation - a creation where sin, death, and the devil are no more and only the Lord and His people remain. And He and His people will live together in a restored, perfect creation, just as God has planned from eternity, and just as He created us to be.

However, this message is offensive to some. It

is "Good News," but not everyone takes it as the Gospel that it is. It is offensive to those who wish to take credit for their own salvation and who wish to rely on their own works to be saved. They find fault with God and the way He acts - God doesn't seem reasonable. They are those whom Jesus rebukes, saying, "We played the flute for you, and you did not dance; we sang a dirge, and you did not mourn." For in Jesus' day they found fault with John the Baptist's message of repentance, his preaching of God's Law. They didn't like the funeral dirge of the Law and they did not mourn of their sins. And they also found fault with Jesus' message of grace, his proclamation of the Gospel in his name. They did not dance to the flute of God's mercy which is given freely through Christ. So, neither Law nor Gospel resonates with those who do not fear God and who do not wish to give him glory; for they want the glory instead and they have turned themselves into their own gods.

Sadly, this type of people overtook the Church for many centuries - the violent took it by force. The Church was covered over with the dark pall of works-righteousness; the deadly, tempting belief that we can earn our way into heaven. It is tempting because it offers us the chance to claim credit and glory for our salvation. But it is deadly, because the requirement to get into heaven - "fear God and keep his commandments" - is something we just can not do. However, this deadly cloud hung over the Church for hundreds of years as it built its large monasteries, huge buildings, and ornate cathedrals at a time when its people were dying apart from God. The Church had forgotten its first love - Christ. She had forsaken her husband and had gone whoring after other gods -

wisdom, power, wealth, and pleasure.

But, the Gospel is eternal, because God has planned it from the beginning, He will bring it to completion, and His grace will endure forever through Christ (cf. Revelation 14:6). So, there have always been those in the Church who have continued to call the Church back to faithfulness to her husband, Christ. The Church is called to abandon its false gods of wisdom, power, wealth, and pleasure, and turn to the Lord instead, and fear Him only and give Him glory.

So, not everyone mourns at the dirge of God's judgment through the Law and not everyone dances at the playing of the flute of the Gospel. That is, not everyone acknowledges their sins and thrusts themselves at the mercy of God. Not everyone turns from their idols to the one true God, because their idols are themselves - for by trusting in their own works and possessions to be saved they became as their own gods. This was the original temptation of Satan to Adam and Eve, and many people fall into it. Thus, since they do not mourn at the death dirge sounded by God's Law, they also do not dance and rejoice at the playing of the sweet music of the Gospel. The flute of God's grace through Christ has no impact on those with dull ears, people who can no longer hear the Law or the Gospel, because their senses have been dulled to the message of repentance and grace.

Even so, against all opposition, the power of the Gospel of Jesus Christ overcomes sin, death, and the devil, just as it always has and will do - for the Gospel is eternal, but sin, death, and the devil will pass away. So, God has done it all, and He is with

His Church. He continually raises up people to proclaim His Word to a new generation, just as He raised up Seth after the death of Abel, Noah in the time of the flood, Elijah, Elisha, and all the prophets of the Old Testament, and all the apostles of the New Testament. He has raised up faithful witnesses to His Word from the time of Christ until now, and will continue to do so until Christ returns.

So, those of the Church are heirs of this eternal Gospel. This "Good News" is the Word of God that He has saved us from our sins and reconciled us to Himself through the death and resurrection of His Son; this is the Gospel, the Good News that is to be proclaimed to all people. The Son has set us free, and we are free indeed, because God has done it. We are saved by the power of God, and so we can be sure that our salvation is sure, because God has already won the victory through Christ.

The people of the Church stand as descendants of the long line of the faithful who look to Christ for salvation - a line going all the way back from the New Testament through the Old Testament to Adam and Eve. For after their fall, God promised Adam and Eve a savior (Genesis 3:15) and that promise has been fulfilled. And those in the Church are witnesses to the eternal Gospel, called to go out into the world to proclaim Christ to those who do not know Him. The Church comes to them with the keys that will set them free from their bondage to sin, because the Church has the Gospel of Jesus Christ. Thus, as witnesses, those in the Church in our own time stand in the line of all those faithful saints of God who have gone before us, and who will come after us, who also share this witness to Christ.

And one day we will all stand together. For when Christ returns, he will raise up all those who have gone before and join them with those still living. All the faithful will then be joined with Christ to inherit the kingdom of heaven, the new creation. On that day we will join together in the hymn of all creation, rejoicing that our salvation has come. And this communion of saints will be brought into the presence of the eternal, almighty Lord God to dwell with Him forever in the new heaven and new earth (Revelation 21:1).

We know that in this life we will encounter sin, death, and the devil, but we also know that these will pass away and will be no more. And we know that "God is our refuge and strength, a very present help in trouble. Therefore we will not fear though the earth gives way, though the mountains be moved into the heart of the sea, though its waters roar and foam, though the mountains tremble at its swelling" (Psalm 46).

No, we will not fear, because we know that "There is a river whose streams make glad the city of God, the holy habitation of the Most High. God is in the midst of her; she shall not be moved" (Psalm 46). This city is where we are destined to dwell, drinking from the river of eternal life in the presence of the Lord and His people forever in the new, restored creation. Amen.

# 8 LIFE AND DEATH

## Guiding Passages

Isaiah 25:6-9

*On this mountain the LORD of hosts will make for all peoples a feast of rich food, a feast of well-aged wine, of rich food full of marrow, of aged wine well refined.*

*And he will swallow up on this mountain the covering that is cast over all peoples, the veil that is spread over all nations.*

*He will swallow up death forever; and the Lord God will wipe away tears from all faces, and the reproach of his people he will take away from all the earth, for the Lord has spoken.*

*It will be said on that day, "Behold, this is our God; we have waited for him, that he might save us. This is the Lord; we have waited for him; let us be glad and rejoice in his salvation."*

Revelation 21:1-5

*Then I saw a new heaven and a new earth, for the first heaven and the first earth had passed away, and the sea was no more. And I saw the holy city, new Jerusalem, coming down out of heaven from God, prepared as a bride adorned for her husband.*

*And I heard a loud voice from the throne saying, "Behold, the dwelling place of God is with man. He will dwell with them, and they will be his people, and God himself will be with them as their God. He will wipe away every tear from their eyes, and death shall be no more, neither shall there be mourning nor crying nor pain anymore, for the former things have passed away." And he who was seated on the throne said, "Behold, I am making all things new."*

Job 19:23-27

*Oh that my words were written!*
*Oh that they were inscribed in a book!*
*Oh that with an iron pen and lead*
*they were engraved in the rock forever!*
*For I know that my Redeemer lives,*
*and at the last he will stand upon the earth.*
*And after my skin has been thus destroyed,*
*yet in my flesh I shall see God,*
*whom I shall see for myself,*
*and my eyes shall behold, and not another.*

## Life and Death

In our lives we each have a role to play. We are called into various vocations, such as husband, wife, father, mother, student, teacher, employer, employee, and many more. In our marriages we reflect what God had ordained in the beginning. For, God created man and woman to join together in marriage and become one flesh, just as He created the Church to be the bride of Christ and thus be the body of Christ. The marriage of man and woman reflects this mystical union of Christ and His Church, as our earthly marriages between man and woman are a reflection of this eternal union.

Thus, we live the life of vocation into which God has called us. We also live the life of faith until the time comes when we are called to rest in the presence of our Heavenly Father, while we await the resurrection when God will raise us up, body and soul, to live in his presence forever.

And so we remember that all things come from God; He created us and bestows upon us His bounteous blessings. And our faith is also a gift from Him, a gift that receives these blessings as the gifts from God that they are and then responds in praise and thanksgiving. We know that God's grace is unmerited and given for the sake of Christ and so we are freed to carry out our vocations of serving others in the sure comfort of this grace.

And what is this grace of God? This grace of God is His forgiveness of our sins, a forgiveness that we did not earn, but rather a forgiveness that Christ earned for us through his death and resurrection. This is the love of our Creator, that He not only created us, but also redeemed us from sin and the death that sin brings. As Jesus Christ himself said, "For God so loved the world, that he gave his only Son, that whoever believes in him should not perish but have eternal life" (John 3:16). Jesus is the Son of God, our living Redeemer, the one who came down to us to save us. And the promise we have through him is the resurrection of the dead and eternal life with God.

This is a promise that God has been making to us since the very beginning. When God created Adam and Eve, the first man and woman, our ancestors, He created them to live in perfect communion with Him and with each other. He walked in their midst in the garden and they dwelt with each other, naked, and feeling no shame, for they truly were one flesh in marriage. However, they soon rebelled against God at the instigation of Satan and brought death - which is the consequence of sin - into the world. No longer could they dwell in the presence of the holy, almighty Lord, for they were now sinful, and no longer could they live with each other in perfect communion, for they were now alienated from each other. But, this was not the end of the matter, for the Lord promised to send a savior to redeem them from sin, death, and the devil and restore them to Him and to each other.

The Lord then carried this promise throughout history through His people Israel - which is the Church of those gathered by God around His promise of salvation. Israel looked to the coming of the savior, this Messiah, who would conquer sin, death, and the devil. God kept pointing the eyes of His people outward beyond the horizon to gaze beyond death, to the coming of the Messiah who would raise them from death to new life with Him.

In the Old Testament book of Job we read about how Job experienced immense suffering and witnessed the death of most of his family, even as he was wracked by disease. But, as he underwent this suffering and looked at the prospect of his own death he declared, "I know that my Redeemer lives, and at the last he will stand upon the earth. And after my skin has been thus destroyed, yet in my flesh I shall see God, whom I shall see for myself, and my eyes behold, and not another" (Job 19:23-27).

This faith of Job looked beyond the death he saw to the promise of the coming of the Redeemer. Job saw and experienced death, but he knew that death was not all that there is; death will not get the last word. For the incarnate Word of God, the Redeemer, is coming to bring his salvation with him. Job knew that although he will die and go to the grave, when the living Redeemer, God in the flesh, comes to stand upon the earth he will raise Job up and Job will behold his Redeemer face to face, because death is not the end for those whom the Lord has redeemed.

The Psalmist saw this salvation of the Lord as well. In Psalm 27, he writes that one day he too will behold the Lord face to face and "look upon the goodness of the Lord in the land of the living," and so he encourages us also to wait for the Lord. For although we cry now, the Lord promises to answer. And He will do so by bringing us into His land, the land of the living to dwell in His holy presence as He intended at the beginning of creation.

The prophet Isaiah also saw the coming of the Lord and the new creation. He saw that the Lord will gather His people to Himself and "swallow up death forever." All our pains and sufferings and sins will be no more, for the Word of the Lord has cleansed and healed us, and the waiting will be over when the Lord returns.

The apostle John also saw the coming of the Lord. He saw that the Lord will create a new heaven and a new earth and raise up His people from their graves to live in it. And he saw that the Lord will cleanse his people - the Church - as a "bride adorned for her husband." For Christ the groom will return for the Church his bride and bring her to himself. He will make all things new so that the people of the Church, God's redeemed people, will dwell in the Lord's presence forever.

This, then, is the Christian hope: that death does not get the last word. For we have a mighty Word that conquers death, the incarnate Word of God, Jesus Christ, our living Redeemer. He will return for his people - the Church - and redeem us from death and raise us from our graves to live with him in the presence of the Lord for all eternity. For through his own death and resurrection he paved this path for us and promised that he would bring us with him from death into life through our own resurrections. He promises to return to raise us up from the dead to bring us into the land of the living.

For the death that we now see in this life is not good; death is an unwelcome intruder in our world. It is not what God intended. As we see in the book of Genesis, when God created heaven and earth He intended to dwell with us forever. But the sin of Adam and Eve brought death into the world and alienated us from God and from each other. And so we are born as mortal people and there is no way to escape the death that awaits us.

However, this is not what God intended and is not the end of the matter, for death is our enemy, and God does intend to dwell with us again for eternity. That is why He sent His Son, Jesus Christ, down to us. For Jesus came to prepare a place for us in the presence of God. For through Jesus' death, he died for us. His blood flowed down the cross of his crucifixion to free us from the chains of sin and death so that we may be restored to God. And in the waters of baptism God takes us from the dominion of sin and death and assigns us instead to the dominion of Christ; God Himself brings us out of death into life.

Christ is our Redeemer, and although he died, he yet lives as the firstborn of the dead (Colossians 1:18). He rose from the grave on the third day and then ascended into heaven, back into the presence of our Heavenly Father. Christ is the way, the truth, and the life, because he trod the path we could not travel, the path from death to life. This was Christ's vocation, this was why he was sent: He went before us to prepare a place for us in the presence of our heavenly Father and promises us that we too will travel this path from death to life, due to his triumph over death in his resurrection.

So, although we encounter death in this life, we have the promise of the Lord that death is not all that there is. It is not the end of the matter; it will not have the last word. We know that although we die, we will yet live, just as Christ was once dead, and yet lives. And we know that at the last, Christ our Redeemer will stand upon the earth, and will raise us from our graves, and we shall behold him face to face in the flesh. This is a hope that looks beyond the suffering and death that we now see towards the promise of eternal life that we behold through faith.

Although we now live in a world where there is suffering and pain and death, in the world to come - the new heaven and the new earth - there will no longer be mourning nor crying nor pain anymore, for our Redeemer will stand before us to wipe away every tear from our eyes and death will be no more. God himself will be with us in the flesh and we shall behold him face to face - our great Redeemer - our help in ages past and our eternal home.

So in this life now we have the pledge of that world to come in the Church, God's Israel, those whom He Himself has gathered together as His people through Baptism and the working of the Holy Spirit. God dwells among us now veiled in Word and Sacrament, but on that Last Day when He raises us from the dust and bones we have become and makes us whole again, we will receive the full inheritance promised to us through His Son, the place that he has prepared before us.

For our inheritance, our hope (indeed, our sure hope) is to be raised up from our graves and our ashes, both body and soul, on the Last Day when the Lord returns for us, and we will dwell with the Lord for eternity in His restored creation. The Lord has promised to restore all things and to fix the brokenness we now see through His completeness as God. And He has done all this through Jesus Christ, our Redeemer who although died, yet lives. And in him we have the hope and promise that although we too will die someday, we too will yet live. And this hope is a sure hope, because it rests not in us, nor in our works, nor in our merits, but in the promise of God that finds its perfect fulfillment in Christ. And we know that this promise is sure because God Himself gives it to us, and what a comfort it is that the fulfillment of our hope rests in God and not in us.

For this is the God who created us and who could not bear to see us fall away from Him. This is the God who mourned the loss of us so much that He sent His only begotten Son to us to bring us back to Him. This is the God who sacrificed His Son on the cross to atone for our sins and to restore our relationship with Him. This is the God who brings us to faith in this promise of salvation and restoration through Christ by the working of His Holy Spirit in the Word and Sacraments that He gives to us. This is the God who promises us that Christ will return for us on the Last Day to make all things new and to restore the brokenness and fallenness that, although we now see, will be no more. And this promise is for us, even as it is for those who have gone to the grave before us and who will come after us.

So, as we gather together at our funerals to mourn the loss of those whom we love, we do so with the recognition that the death of our loved ones truly is a great loss and sorrow to us. But, we have something greater than death, and that is the promise of God that He has defeated death through Jesus Christ. Death may win its battles here on earth, but in the day to come, death shall be no more. For the final victory belongs to Christ, and he has won this victory over sin, death, and the devil on the cross, and He has given us this victory as a free gift of God's grace. So, although we die, we will yet live with the Lord for all eternity when he returns to complete all things. Amen.

# 9 HEALING AND COMPASSION

## Guiding Passages

### Lamentations 3:22-33

*The steadfast love of the LORD never ceases; his mercies never come to an end; they are new every morning; great is your faithfulness.*

*"The LORD is my portion," says my soul, "therefore I will hope in him."*

*The LORD is good to those who wait for him, to the soul who seeks him. It is good that one should wait quietly for the salvation of the LORD.*

*It is good for a man that he bear the yoke in his youth. Let him sit alone in silence when it is laid on him; let him put his mouth in the dust— there may yet be hope; let him give his cheek to the one who strikes, and let him be filled with insults.*

*For the Lord will not cast off forever, but, though he cause grief, he will have compassion according to the abundance of his steadfast love; for he does not willingly afflict or grieve the children of men.*

### Mark 5:21-42

*And when Jesus had crossed again in the boat to the other side, a great crowd gathered about him, and he was beside the sea. Then came one of the rulers of the synagogue, Jairus by name, and seeing him, he fell at his feet and implored him earnestly, saying, "My little daughter is at the point of death. Come and lay your hands on her, so that she may be made well and live." And he went with him.*

*And a great crowd followed him and thronged about him. And there was a woman who had had a discharge of blood for twelve years, and who had suffered much under many physicians, and had spent all that she had, and was no better but rather grew worse. She had heard the reports about Jesus and came up behind him in the crowd and touched his garment. For she said, "If I touch even his garments, I will be made well." And immediately the flow of blood dried up, and she felt in her body that she was healed of her disease.*

*And Jesus, perceiving in himself that power had gone out from him, immediately turned about in the crowd and said, "Who touched my garments?"*

*And his disciples said to him, "You see the crowd pressing around you, and yet you say, 'Who touched me?'" And he looked around to see who had done it.*

*But the woman, knowing what had happened to her, came in fear and trembling and fell down before him and told him the whole truth. And he said to her, "Daughter, your faith has made you well; go in peace, and be healed of your disease."*

*While he was still speaking, there came from the ruler's house some who said, "Your daughter is dead. Why trouble the Teacher any further?"*

*But overhearing what they said, Jesus said to the ruler of the synagogue, "Do not fear, only believe." And he allowed no one to follow him except Peter and James and John the brother of James. They came to the house of the ruler of the synagogue, and Jesus saw a commotion, people weeping and wailing loudly.*

*And when he had entered, he said to them, "Why are you making a commotion and weeping? The child is not dead but sleeping."*

*And they laughed at him. But he put them all outside and took the child's father and mother and those who were with him and went in where the child was.*

*Taking her by the hand he said to her, "Talitha cumi," which means, "Little girl, I say to you, arise." And immediately the girl got up and began walking (for she was twelve years of age), and they were immediately overcome with amazement.*

## Healing and Compassion

A few years ago I was up in the attic of our house putting in plywood on the ceiling joists. The idea was to make a surface where I could stack all the stuff that we don't use, but for some reason feel compelled to keep. So, I went up there with a few sheets of plywood and a bunch of nails and a hammer. Normally, when I am in the midst of a project like this, I sort of get "in the zone;" I get in a rhythm.

So, I was holding the nails with my left hand and hammering with my right. Then, when I was nearly done, I hit my left thumb with the hammer. I shook it off and went to grab the nail again, but when I did, I saw that my hand and the nail were covered with blood. So, I finished up in the attic and then went downstairs to wash off my hand and bandage it. I was hoping that my wife wouldn't notice.

But, she did. And she told me that I needed to go to the doctor. I argued with her for a little bit, but I had separated about a quarter of the flesh of my thumb from the rest of my thumb; it was hanging off to the side. So, I figured my wife was right, and we went to the emergency room at the hospital in town. They cleaned the wound really well and put in stitches to hold my thumb together until it healed. They removed the bacteria and put me back together.

At any rate, when I was hurt and injured, I went to the hospital to see the medical doctors. I didn't go to the dentist. I didn't go to the ophthalmologist. I didn't go wander around downtown asking random people if they could help me. I went to the hospital, because I knew they could heal me. The hospital is the place that is marked for healing.

In the text from Mark's Gospel, we see people in a similar situation. First, there is Jairus, one of the rulers of the synagogue in the area of Galilee where

Jesus is visiting. He has some authority and is in a high position in the community. However, his only daughter is dying. No doubt he's already tried the doctors and whatever other methods he could find. But, she's at the point of death and has no hope. So, Jairus comes to Jesus and falls at his feet and implores Jesus to come lay his hands on his daughter, "so that she may be made well and live."

Jairus knows where to go. He knows from whom to seek healing. He goes to Jesus. He doesn't go to one of the fortune tellers; he doesn't go to one of the astrologers; he doesn't go to one of the Greek temples; he doesn't trust in his own works of the Law; he goes to Jesus. He, as ruler of the synagogue, falls down before Jesus in the hope of receiving mercy. And Jesus goes with him to see his daughter.

On the way, a woman is also coming to Jesus. She has another ailment, which the text simply calls a discharge of blood; she's had this for twelve years, the same age as Jairus' daughter. This ailment would have prevented this woman from having children and made her ceremonially unclean in the community. Thus, we see a contrast here. On the one hand we see Jairus who is a well-respected member of the community, a ruler in the synagogue, and who has a daughter. On the other hand we see this woman who has a condition which makes her an outcast and unable to have children.

Now, this woman has tried "many physicians, and had spent all that she had, and was no better but rather grew worse." She was probably embarrassed about her condition, because she tries to hide in the crowd and touch Jesus without him seeing her. She isn't really even supposed to be there, because she could make everyone else ceremonially unclean. So, she doesn't want to ask Jesus for help; she simply trusts that if she touches him, she will be made well.

She touches his garment and is, in fact, made well. She doesn't want Jesus to know that she has touched him, for fear of making him ceremonially unclean. Jesus, though, knew someone had touched him and began to ask and look around to see who it was. The woman then "came in fear and trembling and fell down before him and told him the whole truth." Jesus said to her, "Daughter, your faith has made you well; go in peace, and be healed of your disease." Like Jairus, this woman knew where to go to be healed. She knew who could defeat decay, just as Jairus knew who could defeat death.

Then, after healing her, Jesus and his disciples arrive with Jairus at his house. However, people come out from the house to tell Jairus that his daughter is dead. There's no need to bother Jesus. There's no hope left. But, Jesus overhears and says, "Do not fear, only believe." Then, he takes Peter, James, and John into the house. There are people crying and wailing, and Jesus tells them, "Why are you making a commotion and weeping? The child is not dead but sleeping."

The people laugh at Jesus when he says this. His words sound preposterous to them. Of course the child is dead; they see it with their own eyes. Who is this that thinks she's sleeping? But, Jesus sends everyone outside except for the girl's parents and Peter, James, and John. Then, he takes the girl by the hand and says to her, "Little girl, I say to you, arise." And upon his word, the girl immediately got up and walked, and everyone was amazed. Jesus has raised her from death.

There is a lot going on in these verses. Jairus and the woman afflicted with the discharge of blood are both without hope. Even though they come from different walks of life and are of different social status, they are united in that they share the common fate of humanity - decay and death. But, they know one person who they can go to. They know that their hopes rest in Jesus.

We see in Jesus the power of God manifest, because he is God in the flesh. He is Lord over creation and has the power to restore it. Jesus is our hope when there seems to be no hope, because he is God, and God promises restoration.

Now - to shift gears slightly for a moment - in the Old Testament, the prophet Jeremiah wrote the book known as "Jeremiah" where he foretold the kingdom of Judah's destruction by the Babylonians. He spoke the Word of the Lord that declared that the Babylonians would carry Judah off into exile in Babylon. The northern kingdom of Israel had already been destroyed by the Assyrians and now the southern kingdom of Judah was about to be destroyed by the Babylonians. The entire book of Jeremiah foretells this coming destruction.

Then, when the foretold destruction does come, Judah's hope appears to be cut off. There is no one to turn to. Egypt can not save the people of Judah; it has also been defeated by the Babylonians. Assyria is gone. There is no other power on earth to turn to; except for one - the Lord. You see, Jeremiah also writes the book of Lamentations. The book begins with mourning for the fate of Judah and for the fate of Jeremiah; the prophet weeps for himself and for the people.

However, after reviewing his pain and sorrow, Jeremiah says, "But this I call to mind, and therefore I have hope: The steadfast love of the Lord never ceases; his mercies never come to an end..." Jeremiah knows who to go to; he knows to trust in the Lord, because the Lord will restore. Jeremiah knows that "it is good that one should wait quietly for the salvation of the Lord."

When all other hopes fail, the Lord is faithful and our hopes in Him are well-placed. It may take a while to our eyes, but the Lord fulfills His promises. He promised the people of Judah that He would restore them to their land, and so He did. Likewise, He promises us that He will restore us and the rest of His creation, and He will do this when Christ returns for us. So, we are encouraged to wait quietly for the salvation of the Lord, because it is coming.

In fact, in the text from Mark's Gospel we see what this restoration will be like. Jesus heals the sick and raises the dead. He takes the woman's uncleanness upon himself and makes it clean, and takes the girl's death upon himself and makes life. He is undoing the effects of the fall. Adam and Eve's fall into sin brought decay and sickness and death and all sorts of evil into the world. So, Jesus has come to undo these effects and defeat these enemies of ours. We see him constantly in the Gospels healing the sick and raising the dead, because he is Lord over creation and the new, restored creation that will come with his return will have no sickness or decay or death or evil in it, because Jesus defeated these enemies of his and ours on his cross and empty tomb.

We also see Jesus gathering together all people,

people like Jairus, a ruler of the synagogue, and people like the sick woman, ostracized from society. In the Church, Christ gathers together all people around himself because we will be with him and all the saints in eternity. So, what we see Jesus doing in the Gospels is a foretaste of the full restoration that awaits us.

Here and now in the Church he gathers us together around himself and gives us his Word and Sacraments to sustain us in this life as we wait quietly for the salvation of the Lord. These means of his grace sustain us in our hope until he returns. They give us himself and his Word as we dwell in his presence. But, when Jesus returns for us, he will bring restoration in full. What we see in the Gospels we will receive as well. We will be made whole, we will be made well, we will be raised from the dead. Sickness and death will be no more, because Jesus will cast these out.

Jesus says of all the dead, "They are only sleeping." Many people laugh at this notion that the dead can live again. When the Gospel of Christ is preached, some people laugh, because it seems preposterous. It seems fantastical that one day we will live in a world with no sickness, no decay, no death. Surely the dead will not rise again.

But, "[t]he steadfast love of the Lord never ceases; his mercies never come to an end..." All these things that seem impossible He will assuredly bring to pass. He will heal the sick and raise the dead, and we know this because he's done it before. We see Jesus doing it in the Gospels, and we see Jesus himself rising from the dead. He took all our sin, uncleanliness, pain, sorrow, and death upon himself on his cross and killed them there and then rose to life.  And he has baptized us into his death and resurrection so that we too will share in this new life, a life we have in part now as baptized children of God, and a life we will have in full upon Christ's return.

Many people place their hopes not in the Lord but in many other things in this world.  They trust in money, in ideologies, in people.  They pursue various other religions in an effort to achieve some semblance of peace and healing.  Some people read horoscopes, some people believe in crystals, some people have lucky rabbits feet, lucky pennies, or some other talisman; some people abuse drugs or alcohol.  However, all these other things leave us wanting; they can not fulfill us or heal us.  They would be like me going to the dentist or the eye doctor with a torn thumb when I really need to go to the emergency room.

Thus, other things in the world will fail us. Other things will not live up to our hopes.  But, we know in whom to trust, in whom to hope, and he will not fail us.  Like the woman with the issue of blood and like Jairus, we know that Jesus is the one who heals and raises the dead.  He has pledged this promise with his own body and blood that was given up and poured out for us on the cross and was raised on the third day for us and is continually given to us each week in the Lord's Supper.  The Lord Jesus Christ has done all this for us, because he is merciful and loving and has made us sons and daughters of God.

The Lord is the one who restores us to life from among those who go down to the pit, the one who brings up our souls from Sheol - from the grave - so, "Sing praises to the Lord, O you his saints, and give thanks to his holy name" (cf. Psalm 30). Amen.

# 10 CLEANING UP

## Guiding Passages

Ephesians 6:10-20

*Finally, be strong in the Lord and in the strength of his might. Put on the whole armor of God, that you may be able to stand against the schemes of the devil.*

*For we do not wrestle against flesh and blood, but against the rulers, against the authorities, against the cosmic powers over this present darkness, against the spiritual forces of evil in the heavenly places.*

*Therefore take up the whole armor of God, that you may be able to withstand in the evil day, and having done all, to stand firm.*

*Stand therefore, having fastened on the belt of truth, and having put on the breastplate of righteousness, and, as shoes for your feet, having put on the readiness given by the gospel of peace.*

*In all circumstances take up the shield of faith, with which you can extinguish all the flaming darts of the evil one; and take the helmet of salvation, and the sword of the Spirit, which is the word of God, praying at all times in the Spirit, with all prayer and supplication. To that end keep alert with all perseverance, making supplication for all the saints, and also for me, that words may be given to me in opening my mouth boldly to proclaim the mystery of the gospel, for which I am an ambassador in chains, that I may declare it boldly, as I ought to speak.*

Mark 7:14-23

*And [Jesus] called the people to him again and said to them, "Hear me, all of you, and understand: There is nothing outside a person that by going into him can defile him, but the things that come out of a person are what defile him."*

*And when he had entered the house and left the people, his disciples asked him about the parable. And he said to them, "Then are you also without understanding? Do you not see that whatever goes into a person from outside cannot defile him, since it enters not his heart but his stomach, and is expelled?" (Thus he declared all foods clean.)*

*And he said, "What comes out of a person is what defiles him. For from within, out of the heart of man, come evil thoughts, sexual immorality, theft, murder, adultery, coveting, wickedness, deceit, sensuality, envy, slander, pride, foolishness. All these evil things come from within, and they defile a person."*

## Cleaning Up

A few years ago I happened to meet a county health inspector. As we were talking I said to him, "I bet you don't eat out much at restaurants." And he said, "Oh no way. You wouldn't believe the things I've seen." Then, he proceeded to tell me stories about the strange and gross things he had seen at restaurants during his inspections. After talking with him, it took me awhile before I was able to go eat at a restaurant again.

Basically what the health inspector told me is that he had seen some absolutely filthy restaurants; the kind that you're sure to get sick from. If you go into a restaurant and it's filled with roaches and rat droppings, you shouldn't be surprised if you get sick from eating there. What's inside the restaurant defiles all the things that the restaurant produces.

Now, in the text from Mark's Gospel, Jesus also talks about food. He says that with regards to our relationship with God all foods are clean. That is, it's not what we eat that makes us unclean before God. The Jews were very observant about what foods they could eat and not eat, because they thought that they would defile themselves if they ate certain things. But, Jesus says that this isn't what's important.

Rather, says Jesus, "What comes out of a person is what defiles him. For from within, out of the heart of man, come evil thoughts, sexual immorality, theft, murder, adultery, coveting, wickedness, deceit, sensuality, envy, slander, pride, foolishness. All these evil things come from within, and they defile a person."

As Jesus implies, we are by nature like dirty restaurants. We are filled with unclean things like roaches and rats. And so we shouldn't be surprised that unclean things come out of us, because the things inside defile all that we do. In the case of dirty restaurants these are things like e-coli and botulism; in the case of us, it's the things Jesus mentioned - all manner of sins.

If we expect clean things to come out of us, we need to be cleansed first. We can't expect to produce good things if what's inside is dirty, just as we can't expect a dirty restaurant to produce clean food. So, like a dirty restaurant we need a health inspector to come in and show us all the things that are wrong and then we need a cleaning crew to get things into shape. Only then will we produce good things. No longer will our works be tainted with e-coli and botulism, but instead will be clean and wholesome.

In Deuteronomy chapter four the Lord tells His people to listen to and perform the Law that He is giving them (Deuteronomy 1-2,6-9). His Law is their wisdom and understanding. God uses His Law in the same way a health inspector does his work. God's Law diagnoses what is wrong with us. It shows us what is unclean within us. It shows us that what is inside is what defiles us. It shows us what needs to be cleaned up. What it doesn't do, though, is actually clean us up.  For that we need a cleaning crew.

And this cleaning crew is the Holy Spirit who comes with the Gospel of Jesus Christ.  While the Law shows us what's wrong, the Gospel cleans us up.  The Law shows us that we are defiled on the inside, while the Gospel deal with this problem.  Through the power of the Holy Spirit in the proclamation of the Gospel, God not only forgives us of all our sins, but also cleans up the mess within us.  He cleans the restaurant, so to speak.  And once He cleanses us by bringing us to faith in Christ, He then works within us to produce good works, works that are beneficial to the life of the world.  He justifies us in His sight and then sanctifies us to produce good works.

So, by nature, we are like dirty restaurants, condemned by the righteous health inspector.  Since we are defiled, all the works we produce are defiled as well.  A bad restaurant can't produce enough pies and bacon to make it worth going there if the pies are rancid and the bacon is green.  Likewise, in our natural state, our works are tainted and we can't produce enough of these rancid works to earn our salvation.  We can't cleanse ourselves.

But, God in His mercy has cleansed us through the death and resurrection of His Son and through the life-giving faith of the Holy Spirit.  He received us just as we are, but we are no longer just as we were.  Through God's Word and Sacraments we have been brought to faith, cleaned up, and enabled to produce good works.  The good, clean works flow from what God has first done for us and to us.  He's cleansed us in the waters of Baptism and made us His own, so what we now produce flows out from this new identity in Christ.

This is Paul's point in Ephesians. We have been saved; we have been redeemed from the power of sin, death, and the devil; we have been cleansed. Therefore, "be strong in the Lord and in the strength of His might. Put on the whole armor of God, that you may be able to stand against the schemes of the devil." Paul then says that the battle is not against flesh and blood, but against the devil and his powers. They are like roaches and rats that want to come back in to the restaurant to infect it and make it what it once was. They want us to go back to what we once were.

Thus, just like a restaurant needs to be continually cleansed to keep it clean and fumigated to keep out roaches and rats, so too do we need to be continually guarded against the infestations of evil that are always waiting to infect us. Paul says to put on the belt of truth, the breastplate of righteousness, the ready shoes of the Gospel, the shield of faith, the helmet of salvation, and the sword of the Word of God by which the Holy Spirit works. Once gilded with all these armaments, we are to pray and keep alert and guard against the power of evil.

And we do this by continually receiving God's gifts in Word and Sacrament. If we neglect these gifts of His to us, we should not be surprised that we fall back into the way we once were. We should not be surprised that we again become as unclean restaurants, producing unclean works.

So, we have a continual need to come before the Lord to receive His gifts by which He continually cleanses us, for He has promised to work through His Word and Sacraments. When we were Baptized, the Lord cleansed us by uniting us with Christ's own baptism, his death and resurrection. But, just as you don't clean a restaurant and then leave it be, but rather must continually keep up the maintenance, so too does the Lord not leave us be to fend for ourselves, but instead continually maintains us in the faith.

To do so, He gives us His Word by which we are kept up in faith and continually cleansed by the power of the Holy Spirit working through the Gospel of Jesus Christ. This Gospel - this Good News - is that Christ died and rose for us. It's a gift; God did it, even though we were unclean and undeserving. We were filthy with our sins, but God graciously forgave and cleansed us of all of them through Christ. God is like the cleaning crew that comes into a condemned restaurant and saves it and puts it back into operation. God has forgiven us, cleansed us, and puts us back into life with Him. And throughout our life, God continually cleanses us with His Word to keep us in faith in Christ, to keep us clean.

And God gives us His Word in a number of ways, because we need to be cleansed with many tools. He gives us His written Word in the Bible: we read about God's promises to Israel, His Church, and their fulfillment in Christ. He has given us His proclaimed Word: we hear the Gospel proclaimed to us about how God in His mercy has made us His children through Christ and incorporated us as His people. He has given us His incarnate Word: we eat and drink the body and blood of Christ that was given up and poured out for us.

Throughout our lives we still struggle with sin. We still have sin, like roaches and rats, that seek to infest us and foul things up. If left unattended, these pests would overtake us. That's why God continually gives us His Word to cleanse us and keep us in faith in Christ.

And then when Christ returns he will clean everything in all creation for the last and final time. He will cast out all the roaches and rats of the devil. He will fully remove all sin and evil and death from the world as he casts out Satan and his servants. And Christ will raise us up, cleansed thoroughly with his righteousness to dwell with him forever. The cleansing that has begun in this life will be perfected with Christ's return so that in the life to come there is no longer anything defiled in all of God's creation. God has promised this to us, has achieved the victory here and now through the death and resurrection of Christ, and will complete the cleansing and restoration when Christ returns for us. Amen.

# 11 CHURCH AND WORLD

## Guiding Passages

Isaiah 66:10-14

*Rejoice with Jerusalem, and be glad for her, all you who love her; rejoice with her in joy, all you who mourn over her; that you may nurse and be satisfied from her consoling breast; that you may drink deeply with delight from her glorious abundance.*

*For thus says the LORD: "Behold, I will extend peace to her like a river, and the glory of the nations like an overflowing stream; and you shall nurse, you shall be carried upon her hip, and bounced upon her knees. As one whom his mother comforts, so I will comfort you; you shall be comforted in Jerusalem."*

*You shall see, and your heart shall rejoice; your bones shall flourish like the grass; and the hand of the LORD shall be known to his servants, and he shall show his indignation against his enemies.*

Luke 10:1-20

*After this the Lord appointed seventy-two others and sent them on ahead of him, two by two, into every town and place where he himself was about to go.*

*And he said to them, "The harvest is plentiful, but the laborers are few. Therefore pray earnestly to the Lord of the harvest to send out laborers into his harvest. Go your way; behold, I am sending you out as lambs in the midst of wolves. Carry no moneybag, no knapsack, no sandals, and greet no one on the road. Whatever house you enter, first say, 'Peace be to this house!' And if a son of peace is there, your peace will rest upon him. But if not, it will return to you. And remain in the same house, eating and drinking what they provide, for the laborer deserves his wages. Do not go from house to house. Whenever you enter a town and they receive you, eat what is set before you. Heal the sick in it and say to them, 'The kingdom of God has come near to you.' But whenever you enter a town and they do not receive you, go into its streets and say, 'Even the dust of your town that clings to our feet we wipe off against you. Nevertheless know this, that the kingdom of God has come near.' I tell you, it will be more bearable on that day for Sodom than for that town. Woe to you, Chorazin! Woe to you, Bethsaida! For if the mighty works done in you had been done in Tyre and Sidon, they would have repented long ago, sitting in sackcloth and ashes. But it will be more bearable in the judgment for Tyre and Sidon than for you. And you, Capernaum, will you be exalted to heaven? You shall be brought down to Hades. The one who hears you hears me, and the one who rejects you rejects me, and the one who rejects me rejects him who sent me."*

*The seventy-two returned with joy, saying, "Lord, even the demons are subject to us in your name!"*

*And he said to them, "I saw Satan fall like lightning from heaven. Behold, I have given you authority to tread on serpents and scorpions, and over all the power of the enemy, and nothing shall hurt you. Nevertheless, do not rejoice in this, that the spirits are subject to you, but rejoice that your names are written in heaven."*

## Church and World

Every year on July 4th Americans celebrate the declaration of independence from Great Britain. We celebrate the signing of a document that condemned the men who signed it to certain death had the American Revolution failed. We celebrate the day a new nation was called forth, one that held that all people were created equal and endowed by their Creator with certain inalienable rights, among these life, liberty, and the pursuit of happiness. Though we usually look back on this event as if the outcome of the revolution was a foregone conclusion, at the time it was very much in doubt and those who participated were few in number and risked their lives in the endeavor.

We see something similar in the text from Luke's Gospel. The Lord chose 72 disciples to go ahead of him proclaiming his word. They didn't go with any visible signs of success; they appeared weak, having no moneybag, no knapsack, and no sandals. The Lord sent them out as sheep among wolves. Nevertheless, they had his Word and the calling to proclaim this to those they met. They were commissioned to spread the Gospel of peace to all who would receive it, and leave the judgment of those who rejected this message to God.

When they came back, they rejoiced that even the demons were subject to them in the Lord's name. They had gone out not with their own weapons, but rather were armed with the sword of God's Word and found it to be all that they needed. Using God's Word they were victorious. In response, Christ tells them that he "saw Satan fall like lightening from heaven." Christ foresees the defeat of Satan on the cross.

We get another view of this event in the book of Revelation. The apostle John sees that "... the great dragon was thrown down, that ancient serpent, who is called the devil and Satan, the deceiver of the whole world—he was thrown down to the earth, and his angels were thrown down with him. And I heard a loud voice in heaven, saying, 'Now the salvation and the power and the kingdom of our God and the authority of his Christ have come, for the accuser of our brothers has been thrown down, who accuses them day and night before our God. And they have conquered him by the blood of the Lamb and by the word of their testimony, for they loved not their lives even unto death. Therefore, rejoice, O heavens and you who dwell in them! But woe to you, O earth and sea, for the devil has come down to you in great wrath, because he knows that his time is short!'"

(Revelation 12:9-12).

Christ's death on the cross and his resurrection defeated Satan and cast him out of God's presence so that he can no longer accuse us. Satan no longer has any hold on us because he has been conquered by the "blood of the Lamb" and the word of our testimony; the testimony that Christ has taken our sins upon himself and bore our punishment on the cross. Christ covers our sins with his righteousness. Thus, the 72 disciples rejoiced that even the demons were subject to them in the name of Christ. They are conquerors due to his Word and cross.

Jesus tells them, "I have given you authority to tread on serpents and scorpions, and over all the power of the enemy, and nothing shall hurt you." It is as St. James says in his epistle: "Even the demons believe - and shudder!" (James 2:19). The demons shudder because they know that Christ has overcome their master on the cross. They know that their time is short and that although Satan continues to howl and growl on the earth, his time will come to an end. They know that they are overcome by the name of Christ. And so, the disciples are ecstatic that they have this power in Christ's name. As Psalm 44 says: "Through you we push down our foes; through your name we tread down those who rise up against us."

However, Christ tells them: "Nevertheless, do not rejoice in this, that the spirits are subject to you, but rejoice that your names are written in heaven." He reminds them that the power to cast out demons is not the ultimate plan that God has in store for them. For their names are written in the book of life due to the blood of Christ, the Lamb of God, that washes away their sins. The power they have on earth is a result of this justification and the Word of God with which they are equipped. It is a result of them being called together as God's people. It is a result of them being the Church.

As Jesus told his disciples, "The one who hears you hears me, and the one who rejects you rejects me, and the one who rejects me rejects him who sent me." We see that the Church does not act under its own authority, but rather with the authority of the Lord. The Church has been armed with God's Word and Sacraments in order to forgive and retain sins, judge doctrine, and spread the kingdom of God. And it does so with Christ's authority, because he - and his cross - is how God reveals Himself to us most fully and completely as a God of grace and mercy - and as a God who shares in our sufferings, even when we do not know why we suffer.

Here on this earth, we will see people reject the Gospel and refuse God's grace through Christ, and we will suffer on Christ's account. How sad is it that some people reject the message that God has freely forgiven them of their sins and will raise them up on the last day to eternal life with Him through the death and resurrection of His Son? This truly shows our sinful nature. It shows that we as people want to be in control of everything. We tell God, "No thanks, I'm ok. I'm basically a good person. I don't need your grace, I've got it all worked out already, you can keep Jesus."

A few years ago, I saw an article about a famous actor who had just died that quoted him as saying that he'll be okay because his credits outweigh his debits. He, like many, many people, was trusting in his own perceived self-righteousness rather than in the only righteousness that can make us free from our sins - the righteousness Christ won for us on the cross.

To this sense of self-righteousness, God replies, "Oh really?" It's like the young man who came to Jesus as recorded in Matthew chapter 19. The man says, "Teacher, what good deed must I do to have eternal life?" Right away you know he's coming from a stance of works-righteousness. He thinks he can earn eternal life through his good works. Jesus replies, "Why do you ask me about what is good? There is only one who is good. If you would enter life, keep the commandments."

Why does Jesus tell the man this? Surely, Jesus knows that no one can keep the commandments perfectly, no one but Him that is, for God is the only one who is good, everyone else is sinful. Yes, Jesus knows this, but the man doesn't, as evidenced by the fact that the man tells Jesus that he has kept all the commandments. When the main said, "All these I have kept. What do I still lack?" I'm sure Jesus must have sighed. Really? You have always loved God with your whole heart, mind, and strength and your neighbor as yourself? You have never placed your hope in something or someone other than the true God, and you have never hated, abused, lied to, deceived, or used another person?

Thus, in response to this man's self-righteous attitude, Jesus tells him, "If you would be perfect, go, sell what you possess and give to the poor, and you will have treasure in heaven; and come, follow me." When he said this, "the young man went away sorrowful, for he had great possessions." What's the point of Jesus' command? It's not that we need to sell all that we have to be perfect; the point is that we can't be perfect. This man was trying to rely on his good works to be saved. When Jesus tried to hit him with God's Law to show him that he was a sinner, the man brushed this aside, saying "All these I have kept." So, Jesus gives him something to do that he knows the man is unable to do. And in doing so, he shows the man that he really hasn't kept all the commandments. He does have another god before the true God - his possessions. He doesn't really love his neighbor as himself - he loves himself as himself. Jesus hits the man with the Law to try to bring him to repentance so that he will trust in Christ's righteousness rather than in his own perceived self-righteousness. And the proper response would have been for the man to recognize his sinful nature, repent of his sins, and trust in Christ's righteousness for his salvation.

This is what Paul means when he writes to the Galatians: "But far be it from me to boast except in the cross of our Lord Jesus Christ, by which the world has been crucified to me, and I to the world. For neither circumcision counts for anything, nor uncircumcision, but a new creation. And as for all who walk by this rule, peace and mercy be upon them, and upon the Israel of God" (Galatians 6:14-16). Paul writes that he will not boast of his good works, his efforts at spreading the Gospel, or in anything else. He will only boast in the cross of Christ, which, although it appears shameful and foolish to the world, is the only way through which we may be saved. This rule of faith makes us new creations and calls us to where the Lord may be found so that He may give us His peace and mercy.

And where is the Lord found? In the Old

Testament, the Lord was found in the temple in Jerusalem. This was the place where He placed His name and where He promised He would dwell with His people. The nation of Israel had the Lord's presence in it's midst. The people of Israel were called together around the promise of the Lord that He would save them from their sins. They were gathered around the promise of the Christ who would come to redeem them from their bondage to sin, death, and the devil.

In the same way, the Church today is where we may find the Lord. God has placed His name on the Church and washed her clean of her sins through Christ; the Church today is the Israel of God, just as the Israel of the Old Testament is the Church. The Church is where we go to find the Lord and where we can be sure that He is found. Wherever we find His Word being faithfully proclaimed and His Sacraments rightly administered, we know that there we have found the Church; no matter how large or small the actual building or congregation may be. For there is where people are gathered around the fulfilled promise of the Christ who has come and in whose midst the Lord dwells through Word and Sacrament.

While we live on this earth and make our way through life we are citizens of two realms, both the civil realm and the Church. God rules over the Left Hand realm of civil government, which He instituted for our benefit, to maintain order in the world by punishing lawbreakers. This is where His Law predominates, where civil government has been given the sword to maintain order. He also rules over the Right Hand realm of His Church, where His Gospel of the free forgiveness of sins through Christ predominates. The sword has no place here, but rather the battle for people's souls is fought with the Word of God.

Thus, as we live here on earth, we are citizens not only of an earthly nation, but also citizens of another nation as well. We are citizens of these two realms, because not only are we citizens of an earthly country, but we are also citizens of Christ's Church. As great as our country may be, we must remember that God's chosen people is the Church which spans all people, nations, and languages.

We even see this distinction in the Old Testament in the nation of Israel. We see that the Church Israel is oftentimes different than the nation Israel. In the book of 1 Kings, we see that Elijah was one of the few people left in the Church Israel, and that the nation had largely rejected the Lord. We also get a glimpse of this even much earlier when God called Jacob to be the father of God's people, and renamed him Israel. Thus, all who worship the true God are a part of the Church Israel, not just the physical descendants of Jacob. Likewise, not all of the descendants of Jacob are members of the Church (cf. Romans 9:8). Rather, what binds the Church together is God's promise of salvation through Christ and faith in this promise.

Thus, the Church, not any country no matter how great, is the city on a hill, giving forth the light of the Gospel to all the world. The Church is where God places His name and promises that He may be found. The Church has the keys to unbind our chains of sin and set us free under the cross of Christ.

We are called forth and forged as the Church, as this peculiar nation of God, through the work of

Christ on the cross. Just as Israel in the Old Testament was brought up out of bondage in Egypt and brought into the promised land across the waters of the Red Sea and the Jordan River, so too are we brought up out of our bondage to sin, death, and the devil and brought into the Church through the waters of baptism. And just as the people of Israel had to wander in the wilderness forty years until they could enter into the promised land, so too do we - as the Church - sojourn here on earth until all is accomplished and we are brought into the promised land of God's new creation, the new heavens and the new earth.

As Isaiah says, the Lord has extended peace to His people like a river. The Church nurses us through His Word and comforts us in our afflictions, just as Christ shared in them on the cross. The Church will endure hardship during its sojourn on earth, but when all is accomplished, she will be joined with Christ her husband forever, and our hearts shall rejoice and our bones shall flourish like the grass as the Lord draws us into His glorious presence and shows his indignation against His enemies and those who opposed the Church.

Unlike earthly revolutions, however, our salvation is a foregone conclusion, because it has already been accomplished by Christ. He has done it all for us already. He has taken our sins upon himself, nailed them to the cross, and endured the punishment we deserved. In return, he has clothed us with his righteousness. This has already been done and is something we need not doubt. This is the promise of God on which we shall rest all our hopes.

Satan, though cast down from heaven and no

longer able to accuse us in God's presence, will therefore seek to make us doubt the fact that our salvation is a foregone conclusion. He will tell us that we're not good enough to be saved, that our sins are too great, and that we need to do something to earn God's forgiveness. Or, he'll tell us that Christ only died for some people, but not for sinners like us. Or, he'll tell us that Christ's death just makes it possible for us to do good works that earn God's favor. He'll tell us that God will send us all to the fires of hell if we don't give Him a reason to forgive us.

To all these things, we say, "No!" We tell Satan that Christ died for all people, that although it is true that we are unworthy and deserve to be damned, that God in his gracious mercy sent His Son to die for us. We tell Satan that God also brings us to faith in this promise of salvation through His Word and Sacraments, that He gives us everything we need to be saved. Thus, although we are weak, sinful, unfaithful people, we know that our God is strong, righteous, and faithful to His promises. Although our faith may appear weak at times, and we continue to struggle with doubt, we know that God will not be made a liar. He will redeem us from sin, death, and the devil and sustain us in faith in this promise to the end. We know that He will raise us up on the last day to bring us into His presence, while Satan and His demons will be cast into the fires that were prepared for them, not for us. So, when Satan comes to us to tempt us with these thoughts, we tell him to go there. We, however, will rest in the sure promise of God given us through Christ.

As the Lord foretold through the prophet Isaiah: "For behold, I create new heavens and a new earth, and the former things shall not be remembered or come into mind. But be glad and rejoice forever in that which I create; for behold, I create Jerusalem to be a joy, and her people to be a gladness. I will rejoice in Jerusalem and be glad in my people; no more shall be heard in it the sound of weeping and the cry of distress" (Isaiah 65:17-19).

We have a foretaste of this new creation today in the Church - the Israel of God, the holy Jerusalem, the city of Zion on a hill that shines the light of the Gospel to all nations. In this city we have been made new creations through Christ as we await for the completion of all things. And this day is coming when the Lord will return and all things will be accomplished. Until that day comes, the Lord will continue to dwell with us through Christ in His Church and sanctify us to do works worthy of His name. Amen.

# 12 WORSHIP AND WORK

## Guiding Passages

Ecclesiastes 5:10-20

*He who loves money will not be satisfied with money, nor he who loves wealth with his income; this also is vanity. When goods increase, they increase who eat them, and what advantage has their owner but to see them with his eyes?*
*Sweet is the sleep of a laborer, whether he eats little or much, but the full stomach of the rich will not let him sleep.*

*There is a grievous evil that I have seen under the sun: riches were kept by their owner to his hurt, and those riches were lost in a bad venture. And he is father of a son, but he has nothing in his hand. As he came from his mother's womb he shall go again, naked as he came, and shall take nothing for his toil that he may carry away in his hand.*

*This also is a grievous evil: just as he came, so shall he go, and what gain is there to him who toils for the wind? Moreover, all his days he eats in darkness in much vexation and sickness and anger.*

*Behold, what I have seen to be good and fitting is to eat and drink and find enjoyment in all the toil with which one toils under the sun the few days of his life that God has given him, for this is his lot.*

*Everyone also to whom God has given wealth and possessions and power to enjoy them, and to accept his lot and rejoice in his toil—this is the gift of God. For he will not much remember the days of his life because God keeps him occupied with joy in his heart.*

Mark 10:23-31

*And Jesus looked around and said to his disciples, "How difficult it will be for those who have wealth to enter the kingdom of God!" And the disciples were amazed at his words. But Jesus said to them again, "Children, how difficult it is to enter the kingdom of God! It is easier for a camel to go through the eye of a needle than for a rich person to enter the kingdom of*

*God."*

*And they were exceedingly astonished, and said to him, "Then who can be saved?"*

*Jesus looked at them and said, "With man it is impossible, but not with God. For all things are possible with God."*

*Peter began to say to him, "See, we have left everything and followed you."*

*Jesus said, "Truly, I say to you, there is no one who has left house or brothers or sisters or mother or father or children or lands, for my sake and for the gospel, who will not receive a hundredfold now in this time, houses and brothers and sisters and mothers and children and lands, with persecutions, and in the age to come eternal life. But many who are first will be last, and the last first."*

## Worship and Work

There was a television reality show on the Discovery Channel that starred a guy named Mike Rowe. Every episode, Mike participates in doing a different job. A lot of these things he does are jobs that none of us probably ever even knew existed. Mike introduces each episode by saying, "I explore the country looking for people who aren't afraid to get dirty — hard-working men and women who earn an honest living doing the kinds of jobs that make civilized life possible for the rest of us."

As part of the show, Mike has done all kinds of jobs. He's been a bat guano collector, a catfish noodler, a septic tank technician, a horse breeder, a roadkill collector, a garbage collector, a shark tagger, a sewer inspector, a pig farmer, a beer brewer, an oyster harvester, an exterminator, a beekeeper, a sludge recycler, a chimney sweeper, a mushroom farmer, an animal handler, a fuel tank cleaner, a shark suit tester, a leech trapper, a maggot farmer, and many, many other things.

Who knew that there were so many types of jobs in the world? As we go about our day, we probably never even considered that there are people shearing alpacas, people cleaning crawfish, people washing the runway paint stripes at airports, and people making bricks and shingles. There are all sorts of jobs in the world, most we never even think about, but each of which makes our lives a little easier or better. Each of the people doing these jobs, in turn, rejoices in his toil and is occupied with joy in his heart as he engages in his given vocation.

In the text from Ecclesiastes the writer talks about how "he who loves money will not be satisfied with money, nor he who loves wealth with his income." No matter how much money we have, we always seem to want and "need" more. If our income grows, we find more ways to spend it. There's never enough. It's like trying to fill a bucket with water when there's a hole on the bottom; the faster you pour, the more that leaks out. So, more money doesn't make us happy or content. But, for the one who enjoys his work, sweet is his sleep.

Now, we all have various vocations. In fact, each one of us has more than one vocation. A vocation is just a role that God has called us into in this life. We may be a husband, wife, father, mother. We may be a parent, a child, a teacher, a learner. We may be an employee or an employer. We may be a reptile wrangler, a goose down plucker, a cloth diaper cleaner, a tofu maker, a soldier, a politician, a lawyer, a contractor, a teacher, a stay-at-home mom, a stay-at-home dad, a grandparent, or any number of other things.

The point is that God calls people into various vocations in life. He gives us roles to play in this world. Our work in our job, in our home life, and in our relationships with other people is pleasing to God when done according to His will. Our vocations are the stations in life that God has called us into; we and our vocations are the ways in which God tends His creation as we carry out the work He has given us to do. Martin Luther calls people engaged in their vocations God's hands on the earth, because it is through people as God's stewards that He cares for what He has made.

So, that is why the book of Ecclesiastes urges us to enjoy what God has given us, accept our lot, and rejoice in our toil. It's because we have work to do that is given us by God Himself. And if we rejoice in it, then we will not much remember the days of our life, because God will keep us occupied with joy in our heart. Life will be a blessing and full of meaning, because we will work in the knowledge that we are helping to tend God's creation. We are to rejoice and be glad in the work that the Lord has given us to do, because it is through us and our work that our Creator takes care of His world.

This is a different message than we tend to hear out in our culture and society. It is different than what we often find in self-help books and on television. This is because there are really three main views of the world that deal with the interplay between what we might call the spiritual and the material.

One view of the world is that there is a ranking between what is seen as spiritual and what is seen as material. In this view, the spiritual is seen as being higher than the material. Therefore whatever is associated with the spiritual is seen as being better, while the material is seen as being lower and of lesser value. This view is everywhere in our culture; it's in self-help books, it's on television talk shows, it may even sound very pious. This view says that if we want to do something important, then we need to do something "spiritual." Whatever deals with the material world is seen as less worthy and less important.

Conversely, an alternative view of the world is that there is only the material world and that there is nothing spiritual. So, in this view only what can be seen, touched, and measured is considered real. There is no hope for life after death, because there is only death. So, in this view, whatever deals with the spiritual world is seen as unworthy and not important.

Now, in these two opposing views, there is not much to be happy about. The first, spiritual-only view basically says that life here and now doesn't really matter, because the goal is to escape from this life and have our spirits freed from our bodies. How often do we hear someone say of someone who has died that they are now an angel in heaven; this type of statement comes from this type of view. Conversely, the second, material-only view basically says that there is only life here and now and that what we have here is all that matters. How often do we hear someone say that death is a natural part of life's cycle; this type of belief comes from this type of view. Thus, the first view discounts the material nature of our lives, while the second view discounts our spiritual nature. What both views share is that there is not much real joy and hope.

However, into this conflict between these two opposing world-views, there is yet a third-view, a Christian view of the world that does bring joy and hope. This Christian world-view upholds both the spiritual and material nature of our lives. This is a view that says that we as people have been created by God as embodied creatures. We have both a soul and a body. God created Adam from the dust of the earth and then breathed spirit into Adam to make him a living being; we as Adam's descendants are also both body and soul. And God also created this world and all that is in it and tends His creation through His creatures. God has given us tasks - vocations - to fulfill in this life so that we can help care for His creation.

What follows from this is that God's creation is good. It is marred by the sin of Adam and Eve, that is sure, because their sin brought decay and death into the world. But, sin, decay, and death are intruders in God's good creation. They don't belong. They're enemies. Sickness and death is not natural. So, God works in this world to care for it until He finally restores it to the perfection in which He originally created it and removes sin, decay, and death forever.

This, then, is the wonder of our vocations, that God has called us into certain roles and uses us as His hands to care for His creation. God is involved in His creation as its Creator through us. He is neither the remote God of the Gnostics who believe that God has nothing to do with the material world; nor is He the idol of the pagans who believe that He is part of His creation. No, God is separate from creation, but He cares for it. He loves His creation, because

He made it; and He uses us as His instruments to help care for what He has made.

So, the shoe shiner, the jelly bean maker, the fish breeder, the barber, the landfill operator, the onion processor are engaged in vocations that God has given them in order to tend and bless His creation. God is involved in His creation, because He made it and He loves it.

In fact, God is so involved in His creation that He sent His only-begotten Son to die for it. Jesus Christ was the first, but made himself last of all. He is the Son of God, the second person of the Godhead, but He died for us and the rest of creation. He defeated sin, death, and the devil - enemies of God's good creation.

Christ lowered himself by being raised on the cross and then raised himself after being lowered into the tomb. This was the vocation of Jesus Christ, the calling that He had from His Father, to die and rise for His creation in order to bless it and begin its restoration. For through Christ's death and resurrection, the fallen, sin-tainted creation is cleansed and restored to its Creator. God is reconciling His creation to Himself through His Son. God is reconciling us to Himself through His Son. This is a work that we could not do, because all our sins are naked and exposed before God, but Christ took these upon himself and atoned for them on the cross.

So, Jesus Christ isn't the pristine, clean, untouched, remote God that some people imagine. He also isn't the "buddy" and "just one of the guys" that others imagine. No, he is God in the flesh who came to die and rise. He engaged in the ultimate "dirty job" by doing the kind of job that makes civilized life possible for the rest of us. Jesus was whipped, spit on, and crucified. He was grimy, sweaty, and bloody. He was dirty. He was sinless, but he took our sins upon himself and died on the cross to kill them there. And then he rose so that we too will rise from the grave, both body and soul, when he returns again on the Last Day for us. Our God got down and dirty in the work of the cross and empty tomb. And He did this for us; it is Christ's work that saves us, not our own works.

We have been made God's own through Christ's "dirty job." God did the dirty work and now has washed us clean through Christ's blood. We are baptized into His name in the waters of Baptism and fed with Christ's body and blood in the Lord's Supper; he is still here working through Word and Sacrament, still working through His creation to bless us and keep us as His own. We have been brought into the promised land, the land where the Lord dwells, the land of Zion, because we have been brought into Christ's Church as children of God and brothers and sisters of each other.

In fact, the Church is the forerunner of the restoration of all creation. For when Christ returns, all creation will be restored and we will dwell in it with the Lord forever, not as angels floating on the clouds, but as people, real people, with real bodies, living with the real Lord God Almighty. We have a foretaste of this now in the Church where the Lord is here in our midst through Word and Sacrament; but on that day that is coming we will dwell directly with the Lord forever, with no sin, no decay, no death, no sorrow, no evil in the world - just the Lord and us his creatures living in perfect communion in eternity.

Therefore, as God's children, we have an additional blessing over those who do not have faith in Christ. We all have vocations, even those without faith. God works through us all as His hands to care for and tend His creation. But, we have an advantage, because we know from whom our vocations come. We can see with every fish we catch, every bolt we turn, every board we nail, every egg we fry, every diaper we change that this work is pleasing to God because it is work that He has given us to do; and by doing it we are helping to care for God's creation. No one else can be a parent to our children, no one else can be a spouse to our spouse, no one else can fill the role that we have been given to fulfill. God has personally called each one of us into the roles - into the vocations - He has given us.

Thus, we can rejoice and be glad in the work that the Lord has given us to do. We have been reconciled to God through Christ and can now work in the world with joy, doing the tasks the Lord has given us. If you've ever seen an abandoned house or building, you realize how quickly things are overrun with weeds once no one is around to take care of it. Likewise, creation itself would be overrun with decay and disorder if we were not here to help take care of it. This was what God gave Adam and Eve to do in the Garden, tend it and take care of it. And now we continue in vocations like our ancestors by also tending God's creation. God made all of this and He doesn't abandon it.

This is joyous work that the Lord has given us to do, to have a part in His creation, and we don't do it for a reward from Him. We have already been freely forgiven by God through Christ and He has made us children of God. This is God's free, gracious gift to us. And so the work that we do flows out of this gift and out of faith in Christ. God's grace and mercy flows down to us through Christ and then our works and mercy flow outward to those around us. So, we can be content in this life, because we know who we are and for whom we are working. We are God's children through Christ and we are doing works pleasing to Him in our vocations.

So, we see that God works through His creation to bless His creation. He works through the waters of Baptism to make us His own. He works through the bread and wine of the Lord's Supper to feed us Christ's body and blood. He works through the spoken and written Word to bring us the Gospel of Jesus Christ. And He also works through us to be His instruments of care and mercy in this world. God is using His creation to bless His creation.

The world is full of people who are not content and who do not know the freedom and peace that is found in Christ. The world is full of people with full stomachs who are not happy. But, into this sorrowful, anxious world we bring a message of peace and affirmation and hope.

The message of peace is that God has reconciled us to Him through His Son; we have peace with God and each other through Christ. The message of affirmation is that the work we do in this world is not all for nothing; our work helps care for, tend, and improve God's creation. The message of hope is that this world is not all that there is. Even as we improve creation through our work, even as we leave our mark, we remember the one through whom creation is most improved and who made the biggest, eternal mark. We remember Jesus Christ and the promise of God that will be realized in him when he returns.

When Christ returns all creation will be restored and perfected, including us. And we, both body and soul, will then dwell in the presence of the Lord forever and enter into His eternal Sabbath rest. So, we are to keep our eyes focused outward to the horizon for the coming of that hope. And until that day dawns, we rejoice and are glad in the work the Lord has given us to do here and now; and we know that He has given us an important role to play as He cares for His creation through us until the day when He will restore it fully at Christ's return. Thus, our whole lives are lives of worship as we respond through our vocations to what the Lord has done for us through Christ. We are the Lord's hands, called to be hands of love and grace and mercy in the world as we witness to His love and grace and mercy through Christ. Amen.

# 13 LIFE IN THE WORLD

## Guiding Passages

Exodus 20:1-17

*And God spoke all these words, saying,*

*"I am the LORD your God, who brought you out of the land of Egypt, out of the house of slavery.*

*You shall have no other gods before me. You shall not make for yourself a carved image, or any likeness of anything that is in heaven above, or that is in the earth beneath, or that is in the water under the earth. You shall not bow down to them or serve them, for I the LORD your God am a jealous God, visiting the iniquity of the fathers on the children to the third and the fourth generation of those who hate me, but showing steadfast love to thousands of those who love me and keep my commandments.*

*You shall not take the name of the LORD your God in vain, for the LORD will not hold him guiltless who takes his name in vain.*

*Remember the Sabbath day, to keep it holy. Six days you shall labor, and do all your work, but the seventh day is a Sabbath to the LORD your God. On it you shall not do any work, you, or your son, or your daughter, your male servant, or your female servant, or your livestock, or the sojourner who is within your gates. For in six days the LORD made heaven and earth, the sea, and all that is in them, and rested the seventh day. Therefore the LORD blessed the Sabbath day and made it holy.*

*Honor your father and your mother, that your days may be long in the land that the LORD your God is giving you.*

*You shall not murder.*

*You shall not commit adultery.*

*You shall not steal.*

*You shall not bear false witness against your neighbor.*

*You shall not covet your neighbor's house;*

*you shall not covet your neighbor's wife, or his male servant, or his female servant, or his ox, or his donkey, or anything that is your neighbor's."*

## 1 Corinthians 1:18-31

*For the word of the cross is folly to those who are perishing, but to us who are being saved it is the power of God.*

*For it is written,*

*"I will destroy the wisdom of the wise,
and the discernment of the discerning I will thwart."*

*Where is the one who is wise? Where is the scribe? Where is the debater of this age? Has not God made foolish the wisdom of the world?*

*For since, in the wisdom of God, the world did not know God through wisdom, it pleased God through the folly of what we preach to save those who believe.*

*For Jews demand signs and Greeks seek wisdom, but we preach Christ crucified, a stumbling block to Jews and folly to Gentiles, but to those who are called, both Jews and Greeks, Christ the power of God and the wisdom of God. For the foolishness of God is wiser than men, and the weakness of God is stronger than men.*

*For consider your calling, brothers: not many of you were wise according to worldly standards, not many were powerful, not many were of noble birth.*

*But God chose what is foolish in the world to shame the wise; God chose what is weak in the world to shame the strong; God chose what is low and despised in the world, even things that are not, to bring to nothing things that are, so that no human being might boast in the presence of God. He is the source of your life in Christ Jesus, whom God made our wisdom and our righteousness and sanctification and redemption.*

*Therefore, as it is written, "Let the one who boasts, boast in the Lord."*

John 2:13-25

*The Passover of the Jews was at hand, and Jesus went up to Jerusalem. In the temple he found those who were selling oxen and sheep and pigeons, and the money-changers sitting there. And making a whip of cords, he drove them all out of the temple, with the sheep and oxen. And he poured out the coins of the money-changers and overturned their tables. And he told those who sold the pigeons, "Take these things away; do not make my Father's house a house of trade."*

*His disciples remembered that it was written, "Zeal for your house will consume me."*

*So the Jews said to him, "What sign do you show us for doing these things?"*

*Jesus answered them, "Destroy this temple, and in three days I will raise it up."*

*The Jews then said, "It has taken forty-six years to build this temple, and will you raise it up in three days?"*

*But he was speaking about the temple of his body. When therefore he was raised from the dead, his disciples remembered that he had said this, and they believed the Scripture and the word that Jesus had spoken.*

*Now when he was in Jerusalem at the Passover Feast, many believed in his name when they saw the signs that he was doing.*

*But Jesus on his part did not entrust himself to them, because he knew all people and needed no one to bear witness about man, for he himself knew what was in man.*

## Life in the World

The text from Exodus contains the Ten Commandments. It comes just after the Lord, through Moses, has led the Israelites up out of their captivity in Egypt. They are now at Mount Sinai in the desert and the Lord speaks these words to them.

Notice how the Lord starts. He starts by reminding them who He is. And how do the Israelites know who He is? They know Him by what He has done. So, He says, "I am the Lord your God, who brought you out of the land of Egypt, out of the house of slavery." Our God is a relational God, we know Him by what He has done for us. It's like when a parent tells his child, "I am your father, who brought you into the world."

We know the Lord in a similar way. That is why in the Creeds (i.e. the Nicene and Apostles' Creeds) when we confess in whom we believe, we do so using words of relation. We confess we believe in a Triune God who created all things, redeemed all things, and is restoring all things - we confess our belief in a God who has done things, is doing things, and will do things for us and for the rest of His creation.

Likewise, we see this in the Exodus text where the baseline for understanding who this God is who is speaking is what He has done. So, God says to the people that He is the one who redeemed them from slavery. Then, because of who He is and what He has done, He gives the people His holy will for their lives. This holy will is meant to conform them to the plan He has for them, which he told them in the previous chapter, in Exodus 19.

For in Exodus 19, the Lord had addressed the people, again beginning with a reminder of who He is and what He has done for them. He told them, "You yourselves have seen what I did to the Egyptians, and how I bore you on eagles' wings and brought you to myself." This is the introduction, again reminding the people of His relation to them. Then, the Lord continues, "Now therefore, if you will indeed obey my voice and keep my covenant, you shall be my treasured possession among all peoples, for all the earth is mine; and you shall be to me a kingdom of priests and a holy nation" (Exodus 19:4-6).

So, in Exodus 19 we see that the Lord is the one who has created all things and has redeemed this people, the people of Israel, to be His own, a kingdom of priests and a holy nation. They are the Church, called to be the Lord's witnesses and intercessors on earth.

Then in chapter 20, the text quoted above, the Lord gives the people His will for them so that they may faithfully be this kingdom of priests and a holy nation. That is, of all the people on earth the Lord has called this people as His own and set them apart (this is what holy means) as His witnesses on earth, bearing His Word to others and interceding for them before Him (this is what it means to be a priest).

So this is the Church, a kingdom of priests and a holy nation. In the Old Testament we call this Church Israel. Now in the New Testament, we call it simply the Christian Church, but it's the new Israel, because the faith of the Old Testament Church and the faith of the New Testament Church is the same faith, a faith that rests in Christ. In the Old Testament this faith looked forward to the Christ who was to come, and in the New this faith looks back to the Christ who has come, but it's the same Christ who is the center of all the Scriptures and to whom the Lord's people look for salvation.

Thus, in light of what the Lord has done for us in redeeming us, in Exodus 20 the Lord gives His people His will for our lives in this world.

First, He says, "You shall have no other gods before me." And what follows is an explanation of this commandment; don't carve images for yourself to worship - that is do not make anything in creation into a god, because the Lord God is the Creator of all things and is separate from His creation.

Worshipping created things makes these things into a person's god, which is an idol. People use idols, because idols function in a vending machine sort of way. That is, you do the right things, speak the right incantation, give the right sacrifice, and the idol responds in a predictable way, a way that seems reasonable to us. Idols put us in control and cater to our desire to be our own gods. So, today, in this current age, we have idols of money, power, pleasure, or people that we tend to look to for all good things. But, the Lord in this first and greatest commandment tells us that we are to love Him with all our heart, soul, and mind and look to Him only for all good things, because He is the Lord God who created us, then redeemed us from slavery to sin, death, and the devil.

Then, following on this commandment, the Lord says that since He is to be our only God, "You shall not take the name of the Lord your God in vain, for the Lord will not hold him guiltless who takes his name in vain." What does this mean? For one, it means that we are not to use the Lord's name as a curse or swear word, because it is His name and not an object for us to use as we see fit. But, it also means more than this. It means that we are not to use the Lord's name as a cover for our actions; again, the Lord's name is His own and not at our disposal. What this means is that we are not to swear by the

Lord, use His name superstitiously, or use His name to deceive others. We are His witnesses on earth, and so we are to bear His name as He meant it to be used.

Thus, we are to call upon Him in prayer, give praise to Him, and thank Him for all He has done for us, and in so doing be His witnesses - His priests - to the surrounding nations. For we are His chosen people - His Church, His new Israel - and we are priests and a holy nation. We are bearers of His name, "Christians," and therefore have no need to curse or use the Lord's name in vain. Instead, as Jesus says to us in the Sermon on the Mount in Matthew's Gospel, "Let what you say be simply Yes or No; anything more than this comes from evil" (Matthew 5:37).

Then, the Lord gives us the third commandment: "Remember the Sabbath day, to keep it holy." He explains this commandment in reference to the order of creation, for the Lord God created all things during six days, but rested on the seventh. So, we too are to have a time of rest from work, us and our workers and families. And what are we to do on this day of rest? Does the Lord intend for us to sit around on our couches and watch football? Does He intend for us to sleep all day? No, He intends for us to hear His Word, be with His people, and come to receive His gifts at the Divine Service (i.e. worship). He made this day for us, so that we would have time to receive His gifts that come to us through His Word and Sacraments.

These first three commandments are often called the first table of the Law, and they deal with our relationship with God. Thus, they are summarized in the Old Testament and later by Jesus as "You shall love the Lord your God with all your heart, all your soul, and all your mind." For, this is the essence of what it means to have a God, and is what the one true God, the Lord, Yahweh, "He Who Is," intends for us. He wants us to call upon Him as our only God.

And if we do this, then the following seven commandments flow naturally. For, if we truly love the Lord our God with all our heart, soul, and mind, then we will love our neighbor as ourselves. For, we will not feel the need to disobey, lie, cheat, steal, or covet, because we will be looking to the Lord only for all good things.

So, the fourth commandment is "Honor your father and your mother, that your days may be long in the land that the Lord your God is giving you." Notice that this one has a blessing attached to it. That is, listen and obey your parents so that things may go well with you. Governmental authority derives its basis from this commandment, because the authority of government comes from the delegated authority of parents. That is, people come together to form governments to maintain order in the world, keep the peace, and enforce contracts; these tasks derive from God's created order of parents. So, this commandment is also saying to obey the civil authorities so that our days may be long and blessed. Those who don't obey will be punished by the sword that God has given to the authorities to use to keep order.

Then, following on this is the fifth commandment, "You shall not murder." Murder is really what is meant here, rather than simply "kill." Murder is killing without the authority to do so, and hate is the human emotion that murders in our hearts. So, the Lord tells us not to murder or hate another. But, as we just discussed in the previous commandment, God has given civil government the sword to use to punish evil and maintain order. And this civil government ultimately derives its authority from parents. So, in our vocations as parents and those entrusted with the care of others, we are charged with protecting those under our care. Ultimately, vengeance belongs to the Lord, and He will have the last word on the day of judgment to come. However, in this world the Lord also uses civil government as His means of keeping peace, maintaining order, and enforcing justice.

Now, when God created Adam and Eve, He meant for them to join together in marriage and become as one flesh. Eve was formed from Adam, so by the two of them uniting in marriage they became as God intended, one flesh, man and woman, reunited together. And this marriage is an image of the relationship that Christ has with his Church. Christ is the groom and the Church is the bride; that is why the Church is called the body of Christ, because the Church is joined with Christ in a mystical union that reflects the union between man and woman in marriage. And so to safeguard this divinely ordained order, God gives us His sixth commandment, "You shall not commit adultery." This commandment encompasses not just the act, but the thoughts and desires of the heart as well.

And since God created all things, all things are His. Thus we have the seventh commandment, "You shall not steal." For when we steal, we elevate an element of God's creation to the level that only He should have in our hearts. For stealing reflects the fact that we have placed something else in the position that only God should occupy. Stealing shows that we are looking to part of creation as our god, rather than to the Lord only. For when we steal, we are seeking good from something other than the Lord God.

Likewise, we have no need to put other people down, tell lies about them, or to spread gossip that, although it may be true, is detrimental to their reputation. For we know where we stand in relation to the Lord: He is our God and we are His children. We don't need to put others down to try to make ourselves seem bigger in comparison. We can be secure in our identity as God's children through Christ. Thus, we have the eighth commandment, "You shall not bear false witness against your neighbor." We are not to lie, and even more than that, we are not to gossip. In all things, we are to speak well of other people, even as we would hope that they would speak well of us.

Then, in a similar vein to the prohibition on stealing, we have the final two commandments. Number nine: "You shall not covet your neighbor's house." And then, number ten: "You shall not covet your neighbor's wife, or his male servant, or his female servant, or his ox, or his donkey, or anything that is your neighbor's." Again, not only are we to speak well of other people, but we are to help uphold their property and all that is theirs. We have our own houses, our own property, our own wives and husbands, we don't need to covet and try to take those belonging to other people. Just as we would want them to help us keep that which is ours, so too are we to help them keep that which is theirs. For we have the Lord as our God, and we are to look to Him only for all good things, and not try to take what belongs to others.

In all of these commandments, we see that they all really go back to the central issue of who or what is our God. Everything is really an issue of the First Commandment. If the Lord is our God, then we will want to use and call upon His name rightly, hear His Word with eagerness, love His creation appropriately, and help those whom He has created.

However, we are by nature fallen creatures, due to the rebellion of Adam and Eve, and we are thus born sinful and turned away from the Lord. And we see the results of this in the world today, just as the results have been seen throughout history. In the text from John's Gospel, Jesus, when he went to the temple in Jerusalem, found people there using the temple as a place for trade. They were exchanging money and selling animals for others to buy to sacrifice. The people had forgotten the real purpose of the temple - that is, it was where the Lord promised to dwell with his people - so going to the temple became just something you did because you were expected to. Instead of the people going to the temple to be with the Lord, they went out of a sense of obligation. Did they love the Lord their God with all their heart, all their soul, and all their mind? Did they love their neighbors as themselves?

I don't think they did, based on what we see Jesus do in the text. Jesus overturned the tables of the money changers and made the other sellers leave. The Jews were upset and so demanded on what authority he did these things. They wanted a sign that he had the right to do this. So, Jesus said, "Destroy this temple, and in three days I will raise it up."

They thought he was talking about the building. They must have thought he was crazy, because they said, "It has taken forty-six years to build this temple, and will you raise it up in three days?" This building, this temple, was built by Herod the Great over a span of 46 years on the site of the previous temple in Jerusalem on Mount Zion. The temple in Jerusalem had been the place, ever since the days of King Solomon so long ago, where the Lord promised to dwell in the midst of His people.

But, now, Jesus has arrived at this temple and is pointing to another temple. This Son of God, God in the flesh, is pointing to his own body as the temple. For through his body the Lord will dwell with His people, because it is through the Son that we know the Father. Jesus reveals the Father to us; we know God only through Jesus Christ. And the proof of this is that things happened just as Jesus said they would; this temple he referred to was destroyed and raised in three days. His body died on the cross, but on the third day he rose again from the dead and lived. This was the sign that he promised.

What does this mean then that Jesus is the temple? Well, for one thing, it means that a physical temple in the geographical city of Jerusalem is no longer needed. Indeed, the armies of Rome destroyed the temple in 70 AD, about 37 years after Jesus' death and resurrection. There are many people in the world today - some Jews and some Christians - who think that we need to rebuild a temple in Jerusalem. But, they're missing the point - we still have the temple with us, we have Jesus' body in our midst where the

Lord has promised to dwell with us, His people. And we are joined with him through the Church in the heavenly marriage of bride and groom and are therefore united in one body with him.

This is why Lutherans tend to spend so much time talking about the Lord's Supper. It's because the Church has God in our midst in the temple of His body, given to us freely for Him to dwell with and in us as His people. We don't need a physical temple in the physical city of Jerusalem, because we have a physical temple in the New Jerusalem, in the midst of Zion - for God incarnate is in the midst of His Church in body and blood with the bread and wine. The Christian Church is Israel, the New Jerusalem, the mountain of Zion, where the Lord dwells with us in the temple of His Son. We have the Lord in our midst because we are His people and we are united with him; we are the body of Christ dwelling with the body of Christ in the Lord's Supper.

Now, the text from John's Gospel closes with this interesting statement, "... Jesus on his part did not entrust himself to them, because he knew all people and needed no one to bear witness about man, for he himself knew what was in man."

God knows what is in man. And what is in man is counter to God's Law. Man, due to his fallen nature, is a natural rebel against the Ten Commandments. Even as the Lord says to us, "You shall have no other gods, you shall not take the name of the Lord your God in vain, you shall honor the Sabbath, you shall honor your father and mother, you shall not murder, you shall not commit adultery, you shall not steal, you shall not bear false witness, and you shall not covet" - even as the Lord says this to us

- we tend to want to qualify His Words, and make excuses for our behavior. That is why the Jews turned these 10 Commandments into 613 rules; they wanted to detail every possible caveat.

But, God's Law is actually very simple: "You shall love the Lord your God with all your heart, soul, and mind, and your neighbor as yourself" (cf. Deuteronomy 6:5; Leviticus 19:18; Matthew 22:37,39). This is simply to say, "Look to the Lord God only for all good things and in so doing you will be free to love others as you would love yourself."

However, we by nature can not do this. We are not perfect: we set up idols for ourselves, we misuse the Lord's name, we neglect His Word, we hate, we lust, we steal and covet, we lie and gossip, we cause grief to our parents and to our children. And the judgment of God for this sin is death.

But, because He loves us, the Lord sent His Son, Jesus Christ, to bear the judgment we deserve. Our sins were taken into the temple of his body and atoned for there with his blood, just as the blood of the sacrifices of the Old Testament were taken into the temple to atone for the sins of the people in anticipation of the Christ who was to come to do this once for all people for all time. So, Jesus the Christ died for us, and rose on the third day.

And then, in Baptism the Lord killed us too, connecting us with Christ's death. The person we once were is no more. We are no longer an enemy of God, a rebel against His rule. We are now dead to sin. And also in Baptism the Lord raised us up to new life in Him, connecting us with Christ's resurrection. We are now alive to Christ and connected with all those who have also been baptized into his death and resurrection (cf. Romans 6). We are the Church.

So, now in the Church, we are free to love others as ourselves, because we have the Lord as our God, and we are members of one body, the body of Christ. For Christ dwells in our midst and in us through his body and blood.

So, what of God's Law now? Well, it still serves the purpose it always has, to show us His will for our lives. God's Law shows us what is pleasing to Him. But, lest we begin to think that we earn His salvation through following the Law, it shows us something else as well; it shows us that we can not live up to its demands, we can not be perfect, we are still sinners. So, it drives us to trust in God's grace given us through Christ and the temple of his body, which was given up for our sins and whose blood was poured out for our transgressions.

And to those who are not Christians (i.e. those who do not have the Lord as their God, because they do not trust in Christ) the Law serves another purpose. The Law restrains outward sin, because God has instituted civil government to keep and maintain order in the world.

At its best, civil government is to keep peace in the world so that the Church has room to operate. The civil realm - God's Left Hand - is used to maintain order, while the Church - God's Right Hand - is used to spread the Gospel and thus bring others into the reconciliation that we have with God and with each other through Christ.

Thus, civil government need not be Christian in order to serve God's purposes. Even during the first few centuries of the New Testament Church, when the Roman government was pagan and persecuted the Church, it created room for the Church to operate. It kept peace in the world through the force of its armies, and it built roads that allowed the apostles and the Christian missionaries after them to travel. It fulfilled its task of keeping and maintaining order, even though it was no friend of the Church.

I think this is something we should bear in mind; the government has its role, while the Church has its role, and both are most faithful to their God-given callings when they perform these roles faithfully within the spheres God has assigned them. Trouble comes when either tries to encroach upon the other. We saw that in the Middle Ages when the Church took over the role of civil government and became corrupt. And we sometimes see even now occasions when the government tries to encroach upon the role of the Church. Each has its proper role within God's realm, for God is in charge of all things.

So, we are left with God's Law, which keeps outward order in the world, convicts us of sin, and (for us Christians) shows us the things that are pleasing to God. These are the three uses of God's Law.

We - as Christians - live in the light of God's grace that He has poured out upon us freely through His Son. So, we are free to live lives as God intends, lives lived in accordance with His holy will, in accordance with His Law; not as those who are trying to earn our salvation, but rather as those who have freely received God's grace and seek to live faithfully as the children He has made us.

So, in all things, we do them as a response to God's grace and not out of compulsion. We give, we serve, we help, because God has first given to us, served us, and helped us through the temple of Christ's body and blood. The God we believe in is the Father, Son, and Holy Spirit who has created us, redeemed us, and calls us as His own. Amen.

# 14 LIFE IN THE CHURCH

## Guiding Passages

2 Kings 5:1-14

*Naaman, commander of the army of the king of Syria, was a great man with his master and in high favor, because by him the LORD had given victory to Syria. He was a mighty man of valor, but he was a leper.*

*Now the Syrians on one of their raids had carried off a little girl from the land of Israel, and she worked in the service of Naaman's wife. She said to her mistress, "Would that my lord were with the prophet who is in Samaria! He would cure him of his leprosy."*

*So Naaman went in and told his lord, "Thus and so spoke the girl from the land of Israel." And the king of Syria said, "Go now, and I will send a letter to the king of Israel."*

*So he went, taking with him ten talents of silver, six thousand shekels of gold, and ten changes of clothes. And he brought the letter to the king of Israel, which read, "When this letter reaches you, know that I have sent to you Naaman my servant, that you may cure him of his leprosy."*

*And when the king of Israel read the letter, he tore his clothes and said, "Am I God, to kill and to make alive, that this man sends word to me to cure a man of his leprosy? Only consider, and see how he is seeking a quarrel with me."*

*But when Elisha the man of God heard that the king of Israel had torn his clothes, he sent to the king, saying, "Why have you torn your clothes? Let him come now to me, that he may know that there is a prophet in Israel."*

*So Naaman came with his horses and chariots and stood at the door of Elisha's house. And Elisha sent a messenger to him, saying, "Go and wash in the Jordan seven times, and your flesh shall be restored, and you shall be clean."*

*But Naaman was angry and went away, saying, "Behold, I thought that he would surely come out to me and stand and call upon the name of the LORD his God, and wave his hand over the place and cure the leper. Are not Abana and Pharpar, the rivers of Damascus, better than all the waters of Israel? Could I not wash in them and be clean?" So he turned and went away in a rage.*

*But his servants came near and said to him, "My father, it is a great word the prophet has spoken to you; will you not do it? Has he actually said to you, 'Wash, and be clean?'"*

*So he went down and dipped himself seven times in the Jordan, according to the word of the man of God, and his flesh was restored like the flesh of a little child, and he was clean.*

Mark 1:40-45

*And a leper came to [Jesus], imploring him, and kneeling said to him, "If you will, you can make me clean."*

*Moved with pity, he stretched out his hand and touched him and said to him, "I will; be clean."*

*And immediately the leprosy left him, and he was made clean. And Jesus sternly charged him and sent him away at once, and said to him, "See that you say nothing to anyone, but go, show yourself to the priest and offer for your cleansing what Moses commanded, for a proof to them."*

*But he went out and began to talk freely about it, and to spread the news, so that Jesus could no longer openly enter a town, but was out in desolate places, and people were coming to him from every quarter.*

## Life in the Church

This text from 2 Kings is one of my favorites in the Bible. Naaman is the commander of the army of the king of Syria. Syria often warred with the Northern Kingdom of Israel. For review, after King Solomon's death, about 900 BC, the nation of Israel split into two separate kingdoms: the Northern

Kingdom was based in Samaria and was called simply Israel, while the Southern Kingdom was based in Jerusalem and was called Judah. Syria, based in Damascus, bordered on the Northern Kingdom and at this time, in the mid 800's BC, has an army led by Naaman, who is a leper.

When nations in the ancient world were at war with each other, they would often conduct raids on each other's territory, destroying crops, taking livestock, and carrying off captives. It was a low-order sort of conflict, causing damage to the other side, but without pitched battles. On one such raid into Israel's territory, the Syrians had captured a little girl from Israel who happened to know about the prophet Elisha. Elisha had succeeded Elijah in the office of prophet to Israel, and he lived in Samaria.

So, this little girl became a servant in Naaman's house after she was captured by the Syrians. One day she said to Naaman's wife, "Would that my lord were with the prophet who is in Samaria! He would cure him of his leprosy." So, Naaman, upon hearing that there is someone in Samaria who can cure him of his leprosy, goes to his king - the king of Syria - to seek permission to go to Israel to be cured.

So, the king of Syria gives Naaman a letter to take with him to the king of Israel. This letter implored the king of Israel to heal Naaman and offered up gold, silver, and clothing to the king to do this. Notice how the little girl's message that there is a prophet in Samaria who can cure Naaman is interpreted by the king of Syria and Naaman. They assume that the little girl must be referring to the king of Israel, since he is surely the most important man there. They assume that it's the king of Israel who can cure Naaman. That is why they send him all sorts of treasures; they want to buy this healing from this important man over Israel.

Notice also that the king of Israel thinks that the king of Syria means him as well. The king of Israel just assumes that he's the one that the king of Syria is asking to heal Naaman. That is why he supposes that Syria is trying to provoke a quarrel with him. He believes that the king of Syria is asking him to heal Naaman, and since he can not do this, then it will serve as a pretext for more conflict between Syria and Israel.

Thus, the king of Israel doesn't even seek out a prophet; he just assumes that since he's the most important man in Israel that only he of all people would have the power to do what the king of Syria asks, if only he could. But since he can't do it, then it must be impossible. If the king of Israel can't do a thing, surely no one else could do it either. So, he was distraught and tore his clothes in despair and anger.

But, then the prophet Elisha hears about this and sends a message to the king of Israel telling him to have Naaman come to him, so "that he may know that there is a prophet in Israel." A prophet is one who speaks the Word of the Lord, and people had begun to think that this Word had died out. They thought that the faithless king of Israel held all power over the land. But, Elisha says to them that there is still a prophet in the land; God's Word is still spoken by some.

So, Naaman came to Elisha and stood at his door. Imagine a mighty general, with his horses, chariots, and servants, standing and knocking at the simple door of a humble man.  Here all the world's glory meets up with the hidden glory of God, veiled in flesh and blood.  And Elisha doesn't even come out to meet Naaman.  He sends a messenger to tell Naaman, "Go and wash in the Jordan seven times, and your flesh shall be restored, and you shall be clean."

This simple, humble message angers Naaman.  Here he's come all this way, with his great retinue and great riches, and the prophet doesn't even come out to meet him.  So, he went away angry, saying, "Behold, I thought that he would surely come out to me and stand and call upon the name of the Lord his God, and wave his hand over the place and cure the leper.  Are not Abana and Pharpar, the rivers of Damascus, better than all the waters of Israel?  Could I not wash in them and be clean?"

So, Naaman is angry.  He does not like the word that the prophet has spoken to him.  He expected the prophet to come out and perform some sort of incantation and magic trick to make him clean.  He also doesn't like the fact that he's told to wash in the dirty, Jordan river.  It seems too simple and so preposterous.  The rivers back home in Damascus are better than this simple river.  Surely, he thinks, there's some better way than what this prophet has told me.

Then, Naaman's servants try to speak some sense into him.  They tell him, "My father, it is a great word the prophet has spoken to you; will you not do it?  Has he actually said to you, 'Wash, and be clean?'"

The servants get it.  They understand that although the word may be humble and simple, it is a great word.  The prophet did not give Naaman a great task to perform or ask for all his riches, he simply said, "Wash, and be clean." He was offering free healing, without cost, simply through the means of grace of the waters of the Jordan.

So, after taking the counsel of his servants, Naaman went down into the river, "dipped himself seven times in the Jordan, according to the word of the man of God, and his flesh was restored like the flesh of a little child, and he was clean."

"Wash, and be clean." It is so simple, and is without cost. Thus, to those who are used to glory and honor and riches, it seems too simple and too free. After all, anything that's free can't be worth anything, right? How often do we seek another way, a way that seems better, than the way in which the Lord has told us? How often do we get angry at the Word of the Lord and seek a different way? How often do we hear people say that they don't like the fact that Jesus is the way, the truth, and the life, and they would rather find what seems to them a "better way?" Like Naaman, many reject the Word of the Lord because it doesn't fit with their expectations; salvation appears too simple, too free, because it comes freely through Christ.

We see the act of Baptism in this reading from 2 Kings. In Baptism, the Lord tells us that He is bestowing His Holy Spirit upon us, calling us as His own, and clothing us with Christ's righteousness. It seems too easy, too simple, too "free." We want to do something instead. People buy great hordes of books with instructions on how to be holy, how to achieve salvation, how to be happy, and how to live an abundant life. People buy crystals and candles and other "magical" items in order to be "spiritual." These things appeal to our natural desire for what is flashy and glorious and what is our own work. And yet, the Word of the Lord points us to the humble, simple waters of Baptism, His work: "Wash, and be clean." And yet, many often say, "Is there not a better way? This is too simple, I expected something that really looks magical and profound, not the simple waters of Baptism."

However, the great riches of God are veiled in the humble, simple, free means of grace. In Baptism, the Lord really does kill our old nature - just as the old flesh of Naaman was stripped away in the waters of the Jordan. And in Baptism, the Lord really does raise us up as new creations in Christ - just as Naaman rose up out of the Jordan, clothed with new skin, "like the flesh of a little child." We are born again in Baptism - birthed as new creations in Christ, just as Naaman was restored in the waters of the Jordan.

And it wasn't Naaman's work or the work of the Jordan that made him clean. It was the work of the Word of God attached to the promised means of grace that made Naaman clean. In Baptism, God attaches His Word to the water as His means of grace. If we look to another means, a means that seems better in our eyes, then we are the same as Naaman, rejecting the Word of the Lord because it doesn't fit our expectations or our desires.

In the reading from Mark's Gospel, we also have a leper. This leper comes not to a prophet, though, but to Jesus Christ - God himself. And God incarnate heals this leper with a touch of his hand and His Word. Again, we have the Word of God attached to a means of grace. Jesus touches the leper, and says "be clean." In Baptism, we have this touch of God in the waters and we have His Word which also says to us, "be clean." "Wash, and be clean." The Lord says to us, "Wash in the waters of Baptism and be cleansed of all your sins - past, present, and future - for I have clothed you with the white gowns of Christ's righteousness. You will still err and sin as long as you live, but you are mine and I will save you."

This is why we baptize infants as well as adults, because the power of Baptism doesn't depend upon us; it depends on the Word of the Lord, the promise He attaches to His means of grace. In Namaan's case, the prophet Elisha spoke a Word of the Lord that had a promise attached to the waters of the Jordan. In our cases, with Baptism, the pastor speaks a Word of the Lord that has a promise attached to the waters of Baptism. So, the Lord is the one doing it, not us.

We see this in the Lord's Supper as well. The Word of the Lord has a promise attached to the bread and wine of the Supper. This Word of promise says that the humble bread and wine veils the body and blood of Christ. There is something more than meets the eye; God's Word points us beyond what we see to what He says is there. And this body and blood of Christ in the Supper nourishes the body and blood of Christ gathered around the altar. So, the body of Christ - the Church - is nourished and fed by the body of Christ - the Lord's Supper. The Lord gathers His people around His body that was given up for us and his blood that was poured out for our salvation. This is how the Lord unites His people around Himself, thereby making them His body.

And this is also often rejected by people, even

as Baptism is rejected. We don't understand it, it's too "free," it's too humble, it's too simple. We want a magic trick, we want a hocus pocus act, we want something that appears more glorious than stale crackers and wine. We say: "Surely, I have better crackers and better wine back home! Why don't I just commune at home, that way I don't have to come to the altar with other people; it can just be about me and God." That's what we often want to make it about: "me and God." We think, "I don't need to come to Church, I don't need to be with God's people, because it's all just a question about me. It's about my needs, my desires, my thoughts about what is 'spiritual' and religious."

But, the Lord's Word of promise is not attached to the bread and wine I have at home. Within His Church, He has attached His Word to this bread and this wine at this altar, in the midst of this His people, because this is where He has promised to be: dwelling with His people, veiled in humble Word and Sacrament. So, it's not just about me; it's about the Lord and His people. And He uses his very own body and blood to feed his body, the Church who is united with each other in him.

Likewise, the Lord promises to be in the midst of His people, the Church. The Church often looks weak, humble, and "dirty," just like the Jordan river appeared to Naaman. And yet, the Lord has promised to be with His people: real people, people struggling with sin and illness and conflicts, broken people, people who have troubles.

For this reason, the Church may not look like God's holy people to the eyes of the Naamans of the world. They look to what is clean, bright, majestic, but God points to the lowly flesh and blood of His Church instead, because He formed the Church through the flesh and blood of Christ, just as Eve was formed from the flesh and blood of Adam. The Church is God's people; we are God's people, we are the Church, despite appearances at times to the contrary to the eyes of the world, because Christ has formed us as His own. The restoration of the world that will come with Christ's return is veiled in the humble flesh and blood of the Church on earth.

People often try to find salvation outside of the Church, but the Church is where God promises to be. The Word of the Lord is given and received in the Church, and through this seemingly humble Word, the Lord acts and the Lord heals. So, in all things, the ways of the Lord are not the ways of the world. Naaman sought the mighty king of Israel with wealth and riches to be healed; but, he received healing, freely and without cost, at the Word of the humble prophet by washing in the humble waters. Likewise, many in the world today seek healing and salvation from mighty works or mighty people, but the only way to receive healing and salvation is at the Word of the Lord in His humble means of grace given freely in the midst of His Church. This, then, is how God acts: through the spoken and sacramental Word of grace, the Gospel of Jesus Christ.

So, it's not always the case that what is free and humble is worthless. The love that we have for our spouses, children, family, and friends is free and humble and yet it is priceless, a treasure too great on which to put a price. Likewise, the love that God has for us through Christ is also priceless, a treasure too great on which to put a price, except the body and blood of our Lord and Savior Jesus Christ, who paid for our healing and salvation.   Amen.

# 15 OUR WORD AND GOD'S WORD

## Guiding Passages

James 3:1-12

*Not many of you should become teachers, my brothers, for you know that we who teach will be judged with greater strictness.*

*For we all stumble in many ways, and if anyone does not stumble in what he says, he is a perfect man, able also to bridle his whole body.*

*If we put bits into the mouths of horses so that they obey us, we guide their whole bodies as well. Look at the ships also: though they are so large and are driven by strong winds, they are guided by a very small rudder wherever the will of the pilot directs. So also the tongue is a small member, yet it boasts of great things.*

*How great a forest is set ablaze by such a small fire! And the tongue is a fire, a world of unrighteousness. The tongue is set among our members, staining the whole body, setting on fire the entire course of life, and set on fire by hell.*

*For every kind of beast and bird, of reptile and sea creature, can be tamed and has been tamed by mankind, but no human being can tame the tongue. It is a restless evil, full of deadly poison.*

*With it we bless our Lord and Father, and with it we curse people who are made in the likeness of God. From the same mouth come blessing and cursing. My brothers, these things ought not to be so. Does a spring pour forth from the same opening both fresh and salt water? Can a fig tree, my brothers, bear olives, or a grapevine produce figs? Neither can a salt pond yield fresh water.*

Mark 9:14-29

*And when they came to the disciples, they saw a great crowd around them, and scribes arguing with them. And immediately all the crowd, when they saw [Jesus], were greatly amazed and ran up to him and greeted him.*

*And he asked them, "What are you arguing about with them?"*

*And someone from the crowd answered him, "Teacher, I brought my son to you, for he has a spirit that makes him mute. And whenever it seizes him, it throws him down, and he foams and grinds his teeth and becomes rigid. So I asked your disciples to cast it out, and they were not able."*

*And he answered them, "O faithless generation, how long am I to be with you? How long am I to bear with you? Bring him to me."*
*And they brought the boy to him. And when the spirit saw him, immediately it convulsed the boy, and he fell on the ground and rolled about, foaming at the mouth.*

*And Jesus asked his father, "How long has this been happening to him?" And he said, "From childhood. And it has often cast him into fire and into water, to destroy him. But if you can do anything, have compassion on us and help us."*

*And Jesus said to him, "If you can! All things are possible for one who believes."*

*Immediately the father of the child cried out and said, "I believe; help my unbelief!"*

*And when Jesus saw that a crowd came running together, he rebuked the unclean spirit, saying to it, "You mute and deaf spirit, I command you, come out of him and never enter him again."*

*And after crying out and convulsing him terribly, it came out, and the boy was like a corpse, so that most of them said, "He is dead."*

*But Jesus took him by the hand and lifted him up, and he arose. And when he had entered the house, his disciples asked him privately, "Why could we not cast it out?"*

*And he said to them, "This kind cannot be driven out by anything but prayer."*

## Our Word and God's Word

In the text from the epistle of St. James, he mentions horses. Anyone who has ever ridden a horse, has seen the bit that is put into the horse's mouth to control him. The bit rests in the mouth and on the tongue. The bit then connects to the bridle, and then the rider sits on the back of the horse with the reigns connected to the bridle. So, through the little bit in the mouth and on the tongue, the entire animal can be controlled. That one little part controls the huge beast.

Likewise, says James, are we to control our tongues. If we can control our tongues, then we control our whole bodies. Our tongues are like bits in horses' mouths and rudders on ships; they control and guide us, so we ought to be careful of where they lead us. However, this is difficult for us to do. James says of our tongues, "With it we bless our Lord and Father, and with it we curse people who are made in the likeness of God. From the same mouth come blessing and cursing. My brothers, these things ought not to be so."

Indeed, from the same mouth ought not to come both blessing and cursing. We ought not to come before the Lord in prayer one moment and then turn to other people to curse them. We ought not to gather before the Lord to receive His gifts in worship while remaining at anger with others in the family that the Lord has made us a part of. Out of our mouths should come the fresh water of blessing, not the poison of curses and anger and hate. We must bridle our tongues so that they steer us towards blessing and not cursing.

Sometimes we belittle the power of the tongue. We often minimize the power of words, but words have power. Our words create reality to some extent. If we tell someone that we love them or hate them, those words have an effect; they create that reality of love or hate. If we tell someone that we want to get married or break up, those words have an effect; they do what we say. When someone pronounces a couple as either married or divorced, those words have an effect; they bring together or break up. So, we must be careful to make sure that the words in our lives are blessings and not curses.

So, if our words as fallen human creatures can create reality, how much more so can the holy Word of God create reality. Our words are tentative, they can be weak, they can fail. We can create marriages, but also break them up. We can fulfill promises or we can break them. But, God does what He says and is always faithful to His promises given through His Word. So faithful, in fact, and so powerful is His Word that He created all things through His Word. God spoke the heavens and the earth into existence. And then to redeem and restore His fallen creation from the sin and death and evil brought into it by the rebellion of Adam and Eve, the Lord sent His Word in the flesh, Jesus Christ.

And we see the power of the incarnate Word Jesus Christ in the text from Mark's Gospel. His disciples, even though they were commissioned and empowered by Jesus, are unable to cast out an unclean spirit from a man's son. Their words have failed. Thus, the man brings the boy to Jesus; perhaps God's Word in the flesh will be able to succeed where other words have failed. So, the man says to Jesus, "But if you can do anything, have compassion on us and help us." The man asks for Jesus' help, if he is able.

Jesus says in response, "If you can! All things are possible for one who believes." The man then responds with the faint cry of a grasping faith, saying, "I believe; help my unbelief!"

This is our cry of faith: "I believe, help my unbelief!" We are always in this half-way point of faith; we believe, and yet we do not. We waver, we falter; our faith is not perfect, it is often very weak. And yet, Christ's work and the power of God's Word overcomes our weakness. We see this in the text as Jesus turns to the possessed boy and says, "You mute and deaf spirit, I command you, come out of him and never enter him again." At this Word of God, the spirit left the boy. However, the boy now looked like he was dead; all the life was drained from him through the evil that had possessed him. But, Jesus lifted the boy up and he arose to new life.

The power of Jesus' word, the word of God's Word in the flesh, cleansed this boy and gave him new life. This Word of God, through whom all things were created, is now in the flesh healing through the power of His Word. The boy was mute, his tongue was powerless to heal himself. Even the disciples lacked the power to heal this boy. Man's word failed to bring healing and rescue the enslaved boy from the power of evil and death. But, Christ's Word is strong and able to heal. Christ's Word removed the boy from the power of evil and death and brought him into new life.

Christ's Word creates reality, because He is the Word of God through whom God spoke everything into existence and through whom God is even now continuing to restore and heal all things. This world is fallen and tainted by the sin and death brought into it by Adam and Eve's sin. This world is polluted by the devil and his evil. But, God is healing this world through Christ and his death on the cross and resurrection from the empty tomb.

In fact, in the New Testament we see through Jesus' miracles the healing power of this Word. We see in the New Testament that God is beginning the healing and restoration of His creation through Christ. This healing and restoration was long promised by God, beginning in Genesis 3:15. And Jesus Christ, the Word of God, came in fulfillment of this promise to begin the restoration of all creation. God made a promise through His Word, and His Word came in the flesh to fulfill this promise. The Word became flesh and dwelt among us and died and rose for us.

So, we who have been baptized have been baptized into Christ's death and resurrection and the healing and restoration that it brings. We were once like the mute boy, seized by an unclean spirit, unable to heal ourselves, unable through our own power to set ourselves free. But, Christ has set us free; he has spoken us into salvation. He has removed us from the dominion of sin, death, and the devil, and placed us into the dominion of God instead. He has bespoken us righteous through the power of His Word.

In our Baptisms, God freed us and made us His own by bestowing upon us the Holy Spirit and the benefits of Christ's death and resurrection that He gifts to us. We have been restored to God as His children, no longer rebellious enemies, but rather family through Christ. We have also been restored to each other, no longer alienated, but now brothers and sisters in Christ. We are all one family in Christ Jesus our Lord, at peace with God and each other. This Church of God spans all peoples, nations, and languages, because it finds its unity in Christ.

And in His Church God continues to dwell in our midst through His Word in all its forms. It's not as if Jesus came, died, rose, ascended into heaven, and then left us alone. No, he is still with us. He is ascended on high, seated at the right hand of the Father, but he continues to pour out his gifts to us through the power of His Word brought to us by the Holy Spirit. God continues to work in the world through His Word which sustains us in His Church, the land of the living.

And this Word comes to us in many forms. We believe, and yet we cry out "help our unbelief." We need God's Word to continue to feed our faith. And God is gracious to do this by giving us His Word in so many ways. Thus, we have the written Word, the spoken Word, the sacramental Word; all these forms are giving us the Gospel of Jesus Christ. They are creating and sustaining faith, because God's Word acts and creates; God makes reality through His Word.

God says that we are His own in Baptism, and so we are. Christ says of the bread and wine of the Lord's Supper, "This is my body, this is my blood," and so it is. And he says that this is given for us for the forgiveness of our sins, and so we have exactly what he says we have, freely, as a gift. The Lord's Word has power, and he uses this power to redeem us from sin, death, and the devil, make us his own, and sustain us in this faith. So, the Lord is continuing to build up His Church through the power of His Word, redeeming and making a people for Himself. We may have our growth programs, we may have our plans, but it is God's Word that plants and waters and grows the Church where His peace is found.

Even through we have healing and restoration in this life in His Church, this healing and restoration is not yet complete. What we have here is a foretaste of what is to come. For, this life, this world, is still tainted by sin and evil, and of course we still face our own mortality. But, God's promise is that He will bring the full restoration that Christ began to usher in through his death and resurrection. God's promise is that Christ will return to complete what he started. Christ is coming again, and this promise rests on the power of God's Word, and God always fulfills His promises.

So, the day is coming when Christ is returning. He will complete what he started. No longer will there be the rebellious backtalk of sin. No longer will there be the threat of the grave. No longer will there be the taunts and snares of the devil. Only Christ and His Church will remain, and God's creation will be restored to the perfection and goodness in which He originally spoke it into existence.

We will live with Him in the new, restored creation; and we will be fully restored ourselves. The Lord has spoken us into this promise, and when Christ returns we will receive the complete fulfillment of this promise. The Lord will have the last Word, and we have been sealed into this promise by the power of this Word, so we can be sure of it. Amen.

# 16 OUR CHRISTIAN HOPE

## Guiding Passages

Jeremiah 33:1-16

*The word of the LORD came to Jeremiah a second time, while he was still shut up in the court of the guard:*

*"Thus says the LORD who made the earth, the LORD who formed it to establish it—the LORD is his name: Call to me and I will answer you, and will tell you great and hidden things that you have not known.*

*For thus says the LORD, the God of Israel, concerning the houses of this city and the houses of the kings of Judah that were torn down to make a defense against the siege mounds and against the sword:*

*They are coming in to fight against the Chaldeans and to fill them with the dead bodies of men whom I shall strike down in my anger and my wrath, for I have hidden my face from this city because of all their evil.*

*Behold, I will bring to it health and healing, and I will heal them and reveal to them abundance of prosperity and security. I will restore the fortunes of Judah and the fortunes of Israel, and rebuild them as they were at first. I will cleanse them from all the guilt of their sin against me, and I will forgive all the guilt of their sin and rebellion against me.*

*And this city shall be to me a name of joy, a praise and a glory before all the nations of the earth who shall hear of all the good that I do for them. They shall fear and tremble because of all the good and all the prosperity I provide for it.*

*Thus says the LORD: In this place of which you say, 'It is a waste without man or beast,' in the cities of Judah and the streets of Jerusalem that are desolate, without man or inhabitant or beast, there shall be heard again the voice of mirth and the voice of gladness, the voice of the bridegroom and the voice of the bride, the voices of those who sing, as they bring thank offerings to the house of the LORD:*

*'Give thanks to the LORD of hosts,*
*for the LORD is good,*
*for his steadfast love endures forever!'*

*For I will restore the fortunes of the land as at first, says the LORD.*

*Thus says the LORD of hosts: In this place that is waste, without man or beast, and in all of its cities, there shall again be habitations of shepherds resting their flocks. In the cities of the hill country, in the cities of the Shephelah, and in the cities of the Negeb, in the land of Benjamin, the places about Jerusalem, and in the cities of Judah, flocks shall again pass under the hands of the one who counts them, says the LORD.*

*Behold, the days are coming, declares the LORD, when I will fulfill the promise I made to the house of Israel and the house of Judah. In those days and at that time I will cause a righteous Branch to spring up for David, and he shall execute justice and righteousness in the land. In those days Judah will be saved and Jerusalem will dwell securely. And this is the name by which it will be called: 'The LORD is our righteousness.'"*

## Luke 19:28-40

*And when [Jesus] had said these things, he went on ahead, going up to Jerusalem. When he drew near to Bethphage and Bethany, at the mount that is called Olivet, he sent two of the disciples, saying, "Go into the village in front of you, where on entering you will find a colt tied, on which no one has ever yet sat. Untie it and bring it here. If anyone asks you, 'Why are you untying it?' you shall say this: 'The Lord has need of it.'"*

*So those who were sent went away and found it just as he had told them. And as they were untying the colt, its owners said to them, "Why are you untying the colt?"*

*And they said, "The Lord has need of it." And they brought it to Jesus, and throwing their cloaks on the colt, they set Jesus on it. And as he rode along, they spread their cloaks on the road.*

*As he was drawing near—already on the way down the Mount of Olives— the whole multitude of his disciples began to rejoice and praise God with a loud voice for all the mighty works that they had seen, saying, "Blessed is the King who comes in the name of the Lord! Peace in heaven and glory in the highest!"*

*And some of the Pharisees in the crowd said to him, "Teacher, rebuke your disciples."*

*He answered, "I tell you, if these were silent, the very stones would cry out."*

## Our Christian Hope

The prophet Jeremiah lived during the time of the Babylonian destruction of Jerusalem. He was given a word of the Lord to proclaim to the people of Judah that judgment was coming against them for their sins, just as it had previously come for the people of Israel. After Solomon's death the people of the tribes of Israel had separated into two kingdoms; one in the north called Israel, which had its capital at Samaria and the other in the south called Judah, which had its capital at Jerusalem.

The northern kingdom of Israel had been destroyed by the Assyrians in 722 BC, and most of the people were dispersed throughout the Assyrian empire while other people from the empire were settled in their place. The people called the Samaritans in the New Testament are descendants of those whom the Assyrians settled in the conquered land of the northern kingdom of Israel.

And now in Jeremiah's time, in the $6^{th}$ century BC, the Babylonians are coming for Judah. The text calls them the Chaldeans, because this is the group of people who formed the Babylonian empire, having their roots in the region of what is now southern Iraq. It's the same idolatrous region that the patriarch Abraham had been called out of over 1,200 years before. Now these Chaldeans are coming to Judah to expand their empire. They've already conquered Assyria and taken all the lands of that empire, and now Judah and Jerusalem are next.

It's a scary time for the people of Jerusalem, because the city will be the main focus of the Babylonian attack. Before its final fall in 586 BC, the city would be besieged for two years. And after it falls, the Babylonians will destroy the city, its walls, and its temple; they will also carry off the spoils of the temple as well as most of the people into captivity in Babylon.

So, Jeremiah tells the people of Judah and Jerusalem what is going to happen, but he doesn't leave them without hope. He tells them that judgment and destruction is coming, but he also gives them God's promise of restoration. The city will be destroyed and the people taken away into captivity, but the Lord promises to restore them. The people will learn that Yahweh, the Lord, is not like the pagan gods. He is "Yahweh who made the earth, Yahweh who formed it to establish it - Yahweh is his name." Yahweh is translated as LORD in all capital letters in our Bibles. It means basically "He who is" or "He who causes to be."

This "He who is and who causes to be" promises the people of Judah that He will cause them to be again. He will bring them out of their captivity and restore them to this land that He will also restore. Not only that, he promises restoration to the people of Israel as well as the people of Judah. He promises that he will "cleanse them from all the guilt of their sin against [Him]" and "forgive all the guilt of their sin and rebellion against [Him]."

So sure is this promise that Jeremiah himself,

even though he was the bearer of a painful message of destruction to the people of Judah, bought land for himself in Judah. This is an amazing act of faith. For the land will be overrun by Babylonians and made a part of their empire; they will destroy everything in their path. And yet Jeremiah buys land, because he has faith in the Lord's promise of restoration. Jeremiah's purchase is related in chapter 32. After buying the land, Jeremiah says, "Thus says Yahweh Sabaoth, the God of Israel: 'Take these deeds, both this sealed deed of purchase and this open deed, and put them in an earthenware vessel, that they may last for a long time.' For thus says Yahweh Sabaoth, the God of Israel: 'Houses and fields and vineyards shall again be bought in this land'" (Jeremiah 32:14-15).

This is how sure the Lord's promise of restoration is, that even the prophet who announces destruction buys land in faith in the promise that the land will be restored to Yahweh's people again. And so in chapter 33, the Lord expands upon this promise of restoration. He says that He will forgive the sins of His people, cleanse them of their sins, restore the land, and again make happiness appear and singing to be heard in the land. He says he "will restore the fortunes of the land as at first" and paints a picture of shepherds and flocks and prosperity.

Then, the Lord says, "Behold, the days are coming, declares Yahweh, when I will fulfill the promise I made to the house of Israel and the house of Judah. In those days and at that time I will cause a righteous Branch to spring up for David, and he shall execute justice and righteousness in the land. In those days Judah will be saved and Jerusalem will dwell securely. And this is the name by which it will be called: 'Yahweh is our righteousness.'"

The Lord - Yahweh - promises a righteous Branch of David. That is, he promises that a descendent of King David will come and bring justice and righteousness with him. He will restore the land and it will be called "Yahweh is our righteousness."

Now, in the text from Luke's Gospel we see this righteous Branch of David. Jesus Christ has come in the fulfillment of God's promises. He is descended from David and yet fully God; He is Yahweh in the flesh. And in our text, he is heading to Jerusalem to be crucified for the sins of all people. He will die in order to forgive sins and cleanse us of our guilt. So, as he approaches the city his disciples praise him, saying: "Blessed is the King who comes in the name of the Lord! Peace in heaven and glory in the highest!" The disciples here are echoing what the angels announced at Jesus' birth when they proclaimed, "Glory to God in the highest, and on earth peace among those with whom he is pleased!" (Luke 2:14).

Yahweh has come in the flesh; "Yahweh who made the earth, Yahweh who formed it to establish it" has come to restore the earth. Jesus Christ is Yahweh incarnate, come to restore the land in fulfillment of His promises. So, when the Pharisees urge Jesus to rebuke his disciples he says, "I tell you, if these were silent, the very stones would cry out." The stones would cry out because Jesus has come in fulfillment of all the promises of God to restore all the earth, all creation. The stones would cry out because Jesus is restoring the land.

Our view of what Jesus did on the cross and empty tomb is often too narrow. We tend to think that Jesus died for our sins and therefore we will die and go to heaven. This is certainly part of the significance of what he did, but it's just too small of a view. Jesus did a lot more than this, because his death and resurrection has a much wider consequence. He is the Creator in the flesh who died for his creation in order to restore it to himself.

All throughout the Old Testament there is a huge focus on the land. God creates the earth. He places Adam and Eve in a garden that He made for them, in a specific spot of land. He calls Abraham up out of Ur of the Chaldees and tells him to go to a land that He would show him. He promises Jacob that he would give him and his descendants this land that He had first promised to Abraham. He brings the descendants of Jacob, the people of Israel, up out of Egypt to inherit this promised land. When the kingdoms of Israel and Judah are destroyed, He promises to restore them to the land. God continually promises His people land.

Yet somehow we seem to forget about this focus on the land. After all this talk about land, many Christians still think that the Christian hope is simply to die and go to heaven. What about the land? This "small" hope of going to heaven misses the whole first part of the Bible and the focus on the land. The very stones cry out for restoration, because the sin of Adam and Eve cursed all creation. The land is also contaminated and marred by sin and cries out to be cleansed and restored, along with the people who belong in the land. St. Paul picks up this theme in Romans chapter eight where he talks about how all creation is yearning for restoration, because it too was affected by the sin of Adam and Eve. The very stones are crying out!

So, Jesus comes as Yahweh in the flesh and as a righteous Branch of David to restore the land. And this restoration does not all come at once. The people of Judah, after being taken away into Babylon, were eventually restored to the land after Cyrus of Persia conquered the Babylonian empire and allowed the people to return home to rebuild their city, its walls, and its temple. However, life was still difficult and the land was only partially restored. It still awaited a final restoration. The very stones were still crying out.

And this final restoration began to be ushered in with Jesus Christ. His death and resurrection has begun the final countdown when the land - all the land, the entire creation - will be restored. But, this final, full restoration is not yet complete. We are in the last days, awaiting this restoration while living in a land that is still contaminated and marred by sin. The very stones are still crying out to be restored.

But, God has established His advance teams on the earth. The land is still important. We dwell in a restored land in the Church. Each local manifestation of the Church on earth is where God dwells in the midst of His people through Christ. It is the land promised to the faithful. The land is still important, and here in the New Testament era this land is the Church; and it's still "earthly." We can still touch and feel this land and reap its harvest, because we have Yahweh in our midst through the spoken and written Word, the waters of Baptism, and the bread and wine of the Lord's Supper. This is the harvest of the land, and it is plentiful.

And have you ever wondered why it's bread

and wine in the Lord's Supper? Why not just plain grain and grapes? Bread and wine show the fruitfulness of the land and the vocational creativity of the people in using the fruit of the land. It shows that the land and its people have been restored as at the first and that the Lord dwells with us in this land. Yahweh is physically present in this land with us in the bread and wine of the Lord's Supper. Christ's body and blood is given to us; a body that was given up and blood that was poured out on the cross in order to restore us to the land. Yahweh is also with us in the waters of Baptism and the proclaimed Word. He is dwelling with us in this promised land, because Christ has promised to be with us always.

Thus, the Church is the holy Jerusalem that is called "Yahweh is our righteousness." This is the whole identity of the Church and her people: that we do not have a righteousness that exists in ourselves because we are sinners, but that we have Yahweh as our righteousness. This Yahweh who came in the flesh to die and rise has given us His righteousness as the covering for our sins. He has forgiven us and cleansed us. Therefore, as His gift to us, "Yahweh is our righteousness." His righteousness that comes to us through Jesus Christ is what restores us and all the land and answers the cries of His people and the very stones.

So, like the people of Judah who were brought up out of captivity into the promised land, we too have been brought up out of the captivity of sin and death and the devil into the promised land of the Church. And like the people of Judah who in that land awaited still a fuller restoration, so too do we await the final, complete restoration, just as they do, even though they now lie in the dust of the earth. We all await the return of Yahweh incarnate Jesus Christ when he will complete what he started on the cross and empty tomb. For on that day the promised land will encompass the entire earth and all creation.

Everything that we have awaited for will then be complete. Everything that the very stones cry out for, everything that all the dead of the Old and New Testament Churches cry out for, everything that we cry out for - namely the restoration of the land and our place in it - will be completed. "Yahweh who made the earth, Yahweh who formed it to establish it" will return for it to cleanse and restore it. And He will bring us into this restored land, this land of promise, to dwell in it forever with Him. Amen.

# 17 TO THE END OF THE AGE

## Guiding Passages

Galatians 4:4-7

*But when the fullness of time had come, God sent forth his Son, born of woman, born under the law, to redeem those who were under the law, so that we might receive adoption as sons. And because you are sons, God has sent the Spirit of his Son into our hearts, crying, "Abba! Father!" So you are no longer a slave, but a son, and if a son, then an heir through God.*

Luke 2:22-40

*And when the time came for their purification according to the Law of Moses, they brought [Jesus] up to Jerusalem to present him to the Lord (as it is written in the Law of the Lord, "Every male who first opens the womb shall be called holy to the Lord") and to offer a sacrifice according to what is said in the Law of the Lord, "a pair of turtledoves, or two young pigeons."*

*Now there was a man in Jerusalem, whose name was Simeon, and this man was righteous and devout, waiting for the consolation of Israel, and the Holy Spirit was upon him. And it had been revealed to him by the Holy Spirit that he would not see death before he had seen the Lord's Christ. And he came in the Spirit into the temple, and when the parents brought in the child Jesus, to do for him according to the custom of the Law, he took him up in his arms and blessed God and said,*

*"Lord, now you are letting your servant depart in peace, according to your word; for my eyes have seen your salvation that you have prepared in the presence of all peoples, a light for revelation to the Gentiles, and for glory to your people Israel."*

*And his father and his mother marveled at what was said about him. And Simeon blessed them and said to Mary his mother, "Behold, this child is appointed for the fall and rising of many in Israel, and for a sign that is opposed (and a sword will pierce through your own soul also), so that thoughts from many hearts may be revealed."*

*And there was a prophetess, Anna, the daughter of Phanuel, of the tribe of*

*Asher. She was advanced in years, having lived with her husband seven years from when she was a virgin, and then as a widow until she was eighty-four. She did not depart from the temple, worshiping with fasting and prayer night and day. And coming up at that very hour she began to give thanks to God and to speak of him to all who were waiting for the redemption of Jerusalem.*

*And when they had performed everything according to the Law of the Lord, they returned into Galilee, to their own town of Nazareth. And the child grew and became strong, filled with wisdom. And the favor of God was upon him.*

## To the End of the Age

"Lord, now you are letting your servant depart in peace, according to your word; for my eyes have seen your salvation that you have prepared in the presence of all peoples, a light for revelation to the Gentiles, and for glory to your people Israel."

These words from Luke's Gospel are also found in the Lutheran communion liturgy right after the celebration of the Lord's Supper. They form one of the songs we sing in response to the gifts we've received in the Supper. The song is called the Nunc Dimittis, which simply means "Now Dismiss" in Latin; it's also called the Song of Simeon, because the song contains the words of Simeon which are quoted in the text from Luke.

There's a lot going on within the context in which this text occurs. Eight days following Jesus' birth Mary and Joseph took him to be circumcised. His blood was shed in this procedure in accordance with the Law of the Lord. Then later, since Jesus was the firstborn, they took him up to Jerusalem to present him to the Lord in the temple. And they offered a sacrifice of two turtledoves or two young pigeons. This was a sacrifice of poor people; richer people would sacrifice lambs or goats, but poor people were allowed to sacrifice these birds, since they were inexpensive to buy. So, Jesus' parents had him circumcised at the appointed time, presented before the Lord at the temple at the appointed time, and offered the appointed sacrifice. They did everything according to the Law of the Lord.

And in the temple that day was the man Simeon; "... it had been revealed to him by the Holy Spirit that he would not see death before he had seen the Lord's Christ." That is, the Lord had told Simeon that before he died, he would see with his own eyes the one anointed by the Lord to bring salvation to His people. So, when Mary and Joseph brought Jesus into the temple, Simeon saw Jesus and "... took him up in his arms and blessed God and said, 'Lord, now you are letting your servant depart in peace, according to your word; for my eyes have seen your salvation that you have prepared in the presence of all peoples, a light for revelation to the Gentiles, and for glory to your people Israel.'"

This is quite a faithful response to the Lord's promises. Simeon sees a little baby and declares that in this baby he has seen the Lord's salvation. We might have thought that the Lord's Christ would come in glory; but no, he came as a helpless baby, being carried into the temple by his earthly parents. The Lord truly acts in mysterious ways. The Lord's Christ, the Son of God, came in the humble flesh of a baby. His glory was unseen, being veiled by flesh and blood. And yet Simeon recognized that in this baby Jesus lay all his hopes for salvation. For veiled in this humble flesh and blood was the Lord's Christ, the one anointed to bring salvation.

This is why we sing these words of Simeon after celebrating the Lord's Supper. The Lord has also told us that we will not see death before we see the Lord's Christ. And the Lord has fulfilled this promise in the Supper. He has given us Christ's body and blood in, with, and under the bread and wine. Like the baby that Simeon beheld, we too behold humble-looking bread and wine in the Lord's Supper and have faith that there is more there than meets the eye. Simeon saw past the veil of flesh and blood to see the Lord's Christ; likewise, we too look past the veil of bread and wine to see the flesh and blood and therein the Lord's Christ.

So, the Lord has fulfilled His promise to us. He has shown us and given us Jesus Christ in the Lord's Supper. Christ is our salvation; our own eyes have seen it. The Lord gives us this gift of Christ and the salvation he brings in His Supper. The Lord is blessing us at His Table as He gathers us together as one people of God, the Church Israel.

To echo Simeon's words, this is a table that He has prepared in the presence of all peoples. This harkens back a little bit to Psalm 23 where David speaks to the Lord, saying, "You prepare a table before me in the presence of my enemies." These words of Psalm 23 make me think of the Lord's Supper. For the Church is in the midst of a fallen, sinful world, and yet within the Church the Lord has prepared a table for us where His goodness and mercy follows us and where we dwell in the house of the Lord, here and now in the Church, and hereafter in the life to come forever. For we dwell in His presence in the Church through His Word and

Sacraments, and our own eyes have seen His salvation in the bread and wine of the Lord's Supper.

The incarnate Word of God, Jesus Christ, who is in the Supper gives us His very own body and blood for our salvation. For he is a light for revelation to the Gentiles, meaning all nations, and the glory to His people Israel, meaning the Church. So, Christ is the glory of the Church and a light to all nations.

As the glory of the Church, the people of the Church should speak to the people of all nations about Christ. That is what Anna the prophetess did in the text. She recognized that in this Jesus Christ God was redeeming His people, the Church, and she responded to what God had done for her through Christ. First, she gave thanks, and then she spoke of Jesus to all. She was another person who looked beyond what she saw to recognize the fulfillment of the Lord's promises. She saw the humble baby, and proclaimed him as the Christ.

And yet, although Jesus Christ is God's salvation for us who is given for the redemption of His people, he is also "a sign that is opposed" as Simeon foresaw. Jesus Christ reveals the thoughts from many hearts. We know where people stand with relation to God by the thoughts of their hearts regarding Jesus Christ. Since Christ is the appointed means of our salvation and we only have this salvation and redemption to God through Him, then he causes the rise and fall of many. Those who rise are those whose hearts have faith. Those who fall are those whose hearts lack faith. Christ both unites and divides, joining the sheep together in God's flock, while separating the goats from their midst.

In these two people, Simeon and Anna, we see what faith looks like in God's flock. Faith rejoices that our own eyes have seen the Lord's salvation, faith gives thanks to God, faith speaks about Jesus Christ. Unbelief, on the other hand, rejects the Lord's Christ. Unbelief looks at the baby in the arms of Mary and Joseph and scoffs that this baby could be the savior of humanity. Unbelief looks at the cross on which Christ was nailed and scoffs that this shameful means of execution could be the means of our salvation. Unbelief looks at the tomb of Christ and scoffs that a dead man could rise from the grave. Unbelief looks at the waters of Baptism and scoffs that God could or would act through them with His Word. Unbelief looks at the bread and wine of the Lord's Supper and scoffs that Christ's body and blood could or would be in and with them. Unbelief looks at the Bible as the words of men, rather than the Word of God. Unbelief, in short, scoffs at the Lord's ways, because they don't make sense to our human sense of reason.

However, all these things that seem impossible or at least unreasonable to our thoughts are the way that the Lord has chosen to act for our salvation. He sent His Son in the flesh as a baby; His Son grew up as a baby into a child and then a man; His Son was executed and pierced on the cross; His Son died; and His Son rose from the dead. And just as Jesus was the firstborn of Mary, so too is he the firstborn of all creation - being the Word through whom the Father created all things - and he is also the firstborn of the dead - being the incarnate Word through whom the Father is recreating all things. And God gives us the blessings of His Son in His written Word, His spoken

Word, and His sacramental Word. God acts through His Word to bring us to faith and then keep us in faith, even as He acted through His incarnate Word for our salvation.

St. Paul tied together these refrains of Jesus Christ as the firstborn in his epistle to the Colossians. He wrote of Jesus Christ: "He is the image of the invisible God, the firstborn of all creation. For by him all things were created, in heaven and on earth, visible and invisible, whether thrones or dominions or rulers or authorities—all things were created through him and for him. And he is before all things, and in him all things hold together. And he is the head of the body, the church. He is the beginning, the firstborn from the dead, that in everything he might be preeminent. For in him all the fullness of God was pleased to dwell, and through him to reconcile to himself all things, whether on earth or in heaven, making peace by the blood of his cross. And you, who once were alienated and hostile in mind, doing evil deeds, he has now reconciled in his body of flesh by his death, in order to present you holy and blameless and above reproach before him, if indeed you continue in the faith, stable and steadfast, not shifting from the hope of the gospel that you heard, which has been proclaimed in all creation under heaven..." (Colossians 1:15-23).

This is what faith is then: believing the promises of God that find their fulfillment in Jesus Christ. Believing against appearances and even believing against hope at times. But, faith grasps onto the Word of God that promises that in Jesus Christ we have salvation. Faith is what we see in Anna and Simeon when they look at the little, helpless baby and declare that in him all of God's promises of salvation are fulfilled and then proceed to tell others about this Jesus.

"Now faith is the assurance of things hoped for, the conviction of things not seen" (Hebrews 11:1). There was nothing in that baby Jesus that gave off the appearance that in him was the fulfillment of all our hopes for salvation. The kings of the world wore purple robes and ornate crowns to make themselves look important, but here is the king of kings, the Lord's Christ, clothed in nothing more than the flesh of a baby. And yet, contrary to all expectations, this baby is our savior. He saves us from our sins and the condemnation of death that our sins earn for us. He reconciles us to God, ending the war of rebellion started by Adam and Eve. And not only that, but he is reconciling all creation to God, restoring it to the perfection in which God originally created it.

All this comes through the humble baby presented at the temple by Mary and Joseph. But this baby would grow up. He would grow up to die for our sins and rise from the dead for our justification before God. He would bear the punishment we deserve and fulfill God's Law perfectly on our behalf. He would "[perform] everything according to the Law of the Lord."

And he is still with us now in the Church through Word and Sacrament. Contrary to all expectations, he is in our midst even now in the humble waters of Baptism, the humble bread and wine of the Lord's Supper, the humble words spoken and written for our benefit. And he will be with us always, to the end of the age, just as he promised

(Matthew 28:20).

At the end of the age, he will come again in the flesh for us. He came once as a humble baby, he is here with us now veiled in humble bread and wine, but when he comes again he will come in glory. He will come as the king of kings with all his angels to redeem us, God's elect. And so we have faith in yet another thing which we can not see. We have faith that this Jesus Christ who was born, died, and rose again will return for us. We have faith that all things will then be complete and that we will dwell in the house of the Lord forever in His newly restored creation. For we are the "Redeemed of the Lord" whom He has sought out and has not forsaken (Isaiah 62:12). Amen.

# CLOSING THOUGHTS

It is my hope that this little book provides some degree of clarity and comfort to Christians. Our Christian faith is so much more profound, God's promises are so much more expansive, and Christ's fulfilment of these promises is so much more meaningful that we often realize. God is reconciling all creation to Himself through Christ, and He is ever present with us.

In addition, we live now in the Church with the Lord in our midst, just as did the Old Testament Israel with the tabernacle and temple. God has always been present with His people; He has never abandoned us. In the age to come, we will all be united in eternity when we dwell together in the presence of our holy Lord God forever. The saints of God who have gone before us, those who are yet to come after us, and we ourselves will be raised up to stand before Him when Christ returns to complete all things. All believers will cry out together, "Hallelujah! For the Lord our God the Almighty reigns. Let us rejoice and exult and give him the glory, for the marriage of the Lamb has come, and his Bride has made herself ready; it was granted her to clothe herself with fine linen, bright and pure" (Revelation 19:6-8).

Until that day of Christ's return comes, though, we can take comfort in this present age knowing that the Lord has promised to be with us always, to the end of the age (Matthew 28:20). He has not abandoned us; he is still with us. We are his bride whom he has redeemed from sin, death, and the devil and clothed with his righteousness. We are betrothed to him and await his return when we will dwell with him directly forever. But even now, he is with us through Word and Sacrament; God has always been present with His people and He is present with us now.

Christ has promised to be with us, and so he is. As part of his inauguration of the new creation through his body and blood, he dwells with us - his people of the promise, his Church - through Word and Sacrament. Thus, we have his Word as it is proclaimed to us and as it is poured over us in the waters of Baptism. In the Lord's Supper, veiled in bread and wine, we have the incarnate Word of his body and blood, just as he himself in all his glory as of the only begotten Son of God was veiled in humble flesh and blood in his incarnation.

The Lord continues to be with us in the midst of his Church, just as he promised. He has risen from the dead and dwells with us even now through His Word and His Sacraments. He died for us and he rose for us, in accordance with the Scriptures, because he came to fulfill God's promise to us. And he has baptized us into his death and resurrection for the forgiveness of sins and gift of eternal life and continues to feed us this forgiveness in his Word. He is indeed with us always, to the end of the age; and, in the age to come we will continue to be with him forever. Amen.

"For this reason I bow my knees before the Father, from whom every family in heaven and on earth is named, that according to the riches of his glory he may grant you to be strengthened with power through his Spirit in your inner being, so that Christ may dwell in your hearts through faith—that you, being rooted and grounded in love, may have strength to comprehend with all the saints what is the breadth and length and height and depth, and to know the love of Christ that surpasses knowledge, that you may be filled with all the fullness of God.

Now to him who is able to do far more abundantly than all that we ask or think, according to the power at work within us, to him be glory in the church and in Christ Jesus throughout all generations, forever and ever. Amen" (Ephesians 3:14-21).

# SUGGESTED READING

The following books are helpful resources for Christians seeking to deepen their faith.

Augustine. *Confessions*. Trans. R.S. Pine-Coffin. New York: Penguin Books, 1961.

*Book of Concord, The*. Ed. Robert Kolb and Timothy J. Wengert. Trans. Charles Arand et al. Minneapolis, Minnesota: Fortress Press, 2000.

Chesterton, G.K. *Orthodoxy*. New York: Image Books/Doubleday, 2001.

*Faith and Freedom: An Invitation to the Writings of Martin Luther*. Ed. John F. Thornton and Susan B. Varenne. New York: Vintage Books, 2002.

Forde, Gerhard O. *On Being a Theologian of the Cross: Reflections on Luther's Heidelberg Disputation, 1518*. Grand Rapids, Michigan: William B. Eerdmans Publishing Company, 1997.

Giertz, Bo. *The Hammer of God*. Minneapolis, Minnesota: Augsburg Books, 2005.

Irenaeus. *Against the Heresies, Book 1*. Ancient Christian Writers, Volume 55. Trans. Dominic J. Unger. Ed. Walter J. Burghardt, Thomas Comerford Lawler, and John J. Dillon. New York: Newman Press, 1992.

Irenaeus. *Proof of the Apostolic Teaching*. Ancient Christian Writers, Volume 16. Trans. Joseph P. Smith. Ed. Johannes Quasten and Joseph C. Plumpe. New York: Newman Press, 1952.

Justin Martyr. *The First and Second Apologies*. Ancient Christian Writers, Volume 56. Trans. Leslie William Barnard. Ed. Walter J. Burghardt, John J. Dillon, and Dennis D. McManus. New York: Paulist Press, 1997.

Kleinig, John W. *Grace upon Grace: Spirituality for Today*. Saint Louis, Missouri: Concordia Publishing House, 2008.

Kolb, Robert. *Speaking the Gospel Today*. Saint Louis, Missouri: Concordia Publishing House, 1995.

Kolb, Robert and Charles P. Arand. *The Genius of Luther's Theology: A Wittenberg Way of Thinking for the Contemporary Church*. Grand Rapids, Michigan: Baker Academic, 2008.

Luther, Martin. *Luther's Small Catechism with Explanation*. Saint Louis, Missouri: Concordia Publishing House, 1991.

Luther, Martin. *Commentary on Galatians*. Grand Rapids, Michigan: Fleming H. Revell, 1988.

Luther, Martin. *Commentary on Romans*. Translated by J. Theodore Mueller. Grand Rapids, Michigan: Kregel Classics, 1976.

*Lutheran Service Book*. Saint Louis, Missouri: Concordia Publishing House, 2006.

*Lutheran Study Bible, The*. Ed. Edward A. Engelbrecht. Saint Louis, Missouri: Concordia Publishing House, 2009.

Maternus, Firmicus. *The Error of the Pagan Religions*. Ancient Christian Writers, Volume 37. Trans. Clarence A. Forbes. Ed. Johannes Quasten, Walter J. Burghardt, and Thomas Comerford Lawler. New York: Newman Press, 1970.

Preus, Daniel. *Why I Am a Lutheran: Jesus at the Center*. Saint Louis, Missouri: Concordia Publishing House, 2004.

Tertullian. *Apology*. The Loeb Classical Library, Volume 250. Trans. T.R. Glover. Cambridge, Massachusetts: Harvard University Press, 2003.

Veith, Gene Edward Jr. *The Spirituality of the Cross: The Way of the First Evangelicals*. Saint Louis, Missouri: Concordia Publishing House, 1999.

*Note: All quotes from the Bible are from the English Standard Version (ESV).*

# ABOUT THE AUTHOR

Rev. Aaron Simms is a pastor in the Lutheran Church - Missouri Synod and lives in Georgia with his wife and children. His academic studies include international relations, economics, psychology, classical history, and theology at the Georgia Institute of Technology (Atlanta, Georgia), Troy University (Troy, Alabama), and Concordia Seminary (St. Louis, Missouri).

www.ingramcontent.com/pod-product-compliance
Lightning Source LLC
Chambersburg PA
CBHW070849050426
42453CB00012B/2098